Design and popular entertainment

MANCHESTER
1824

Manchester University Press

general editor:
Christopher Breward

founding editor:
Paul Greenhalgh

Design and popular entertainment

Edited by
Christopher Frayling and Emily King,
with Harriet Atkinson

Manchester University Press
Manchester and New York

distributed in the United States exclusively by Palgrave Macmillan

Published by Manchester University Press
Oxford Road, Manchester M13 9NR, UK
and Room 400, 175 Fifth Avenue, New York, NY 10010, USA
www.manchesteruniversitypress.co.uk

Distributed in the United States exclusively by
Palgrave, 175 Fifth Avenue, New York,
NY 10010, USA

Distributed in Canada exclusively by
UBC Press, University of British Columbia, 2029 West Mall,
Vancouver, BC, Canada V6T 1Z2

British Library Cataloguing-in-Publication Data
A catalogue record for this book is available from the British Library

Library of Congress Cataloging-in-Publication Data applied for

ISBN   978 0 7190 8016 6 hardback

First published 2009

17 16 15 14 13 12 11 10 09 08   10 9 8 7 6 5 4 3 2 1

The publisher has no responsibility for the persistence or accuracy of URLs for any external or third-party internet websites referred to in this book, and does not guarantee that any content on such websites is, or will remain, accurate or appropriate.

Typeset in ITC Giovanni
by Carnegie Book Production, Lancaster
Printed in Great Britain
by CPI Antony Rowe Ltd, Chippenham, Wiltshire

Contents

List of figures

List of contributors

David Attwood worked for the BBC and in consumer research before joining the RCA/V&A MA History of Design in 1993. His MPhil thesis charted the influences of technological modernity and socio-cultural change on the design of the post-war British radio. He is now a freelance writer on design and technology issues. His most recent book, *Sound Design*, was published in 2002 by Mitchell Beazley.

Sir Christopher Frayling is Rector of the Royal College of Art, and Professor of Cultural History there. In addition, he is Chairman of Arts Council England, the largest funding body for the arts in the UK; he is the longest-serving Trustee of the V&A; and he is Chairman of the Royal Mint Advisory Committee, which selects the designs for new coins. He has in the recent past been Chairman of the Design Council, Chairman of the Crafts Study Centre and a Governor of the British Film Institute. Christopher is well-known as a historian, critic and an award-winning broadcaster, with his work appearing regularly on network radio and television. He has published sixteen books and numerous articles on contemporary art, design, film and the history of ideas. In January 2001, he was knighted for 'services to art and design education'.

Beth Hannant is a freelance designer, artist and lecturer in Design History and 3D Design at Kensington & Chelsea College of Art & Design. She graduated from the RCA/V&A MA History of Design in 2000.

Michelle Jones is the Senior Lecturer/Theory Leader for the School of Fashion and Acting Course Leader BA (Hons) Creative Arts for Theatre and Film at the University for the Creative Arts, Rochester. She is currently undertaking her PhD thesis, provisionally entitled 'The English Fashion Industry (1933–1966): The Incorporated Society of London Fashion Designers and Fashion Group of London', in the RCA/V&A History of Design Department. She published an accompanying article to this one entitled 'Design and the Domestic Persuader:

Television and the British Broadcasting Corporation's Promotion of Post-war "Good Design"' in the *Journal of Design History* in 2003.

Josephine Kane graduated from the RCA/V&A MA History of Design in 2002. Since then she has worked as a Live Interpreter for Historic Royal Palaces, and a freelance Education Practitioner in schools and heritage sites across the country, specialising in cross-curricula history and performing arts workshops. She is currently Associate Lecturer on the BA Graphic Design course at Central Saint Martins. In 2007, she completed an AHRC-funded PhD entitled 'A Whirl of Wonders! British Amusement Parks and the Architecture of Pleasure, 1900–1939' at The Bartlett School of Architecture, University College London.

Emily King graduated from the RCA/V&A MA History of Design in 1993 and obtained her PhD from Kingston University in 1999 with a thesis on the design of type between 1987 and 1997. Currently she divides her time between writing and curating.

Dr Nicolas P. Maffei is a Senior Lecturer in Critical Studies at Norwich University College of the Arts. He has published widely on American design in the inter-war period. He is currently working on a book and a major exhibition on Norman Bel Geddes for the Harry Ransom Humanities Research Center, University of Texas, Austin. Since 2001 he has been a member of the editorial board of the *Journal of Design History*.

Alistair O'Neill is Senior Research Fellow & Senior Lecturer in Fashion History and Theory at Central Saint Martins College of Art and Design (University of the Arts London). He is the author of *London: After a Fashion* (Reaktion Books, 2007).

Alice Twemlow is chair of the Design Criticism graduate program at the School of Visual Arts in New York and a PhD candidate at the RCA/V&A History of Design department. She writes about design for publications including *Design Issues, Design Observer, Good, Eye, I.D., New York Magazine, Print*, and *The Architect's Newspaper*. She is the author of *What is Graphic Design For?* (Rotovision, 2006) and *StyleCity New York* (Thames & Hudson, 2005), and has contributed essays to Jonathan Barnbrook's monograph, *Barnbrook Bible* (Booth Clibborn, 2007), *Looking Closer 5: Critical Writings on Graphic Design* (Allworth Press, 2007), *ELSE/WHERE: MAPPING* (Design Institute, 2006), and *Why Not Associates 2* (Thames & Hudson, 2004).

General editor's foreword

When the Manchester University Press series 'Studies in Design' was launched under the editorship of Paul Greenhalgh in 1990 its aim was to provide a much needed forum for work that was developing internationally in the relatively new field of the history and theory of design and material culture, setting design in all its forms within a wider intellectual framework. More than a decade later the series has demonstrated its commitment to this mission through the publication of an expanding list of monographs, edited collections and introductory text books by established and younger scholars whose work has made a real impact on the development of the discipline of design history at home and abroad. A major strength of the series has been its close relationship, through the professional backgrounds of its authors, to the teaching of design history and theory in the universities and colleges, in departments of history, cultural studies, art and design history and particularly in the area of design education. It seems fitting then that this new sub-series of 'Studies in Design' offers a space in which the work of graduates who have benefited from the development of scholarship noted above can find a broader circulation.

In some ways informing and running in parallel with the series, the post-graduate course in the History of Design, founded in 1983 and run by the Royal College of Art and the Victoria and Albert Museum, has also played a pioneering role in defining the territory of design history on an international stage. It has produced many graduates who have since been highly influential in the worlds of lecturing, museum work, retailing, design consultancy and journalism (indeed several have gone on to publish in this series). The V&A/RCA Studies in Design Anthologies offer a valuable overview of the original work that this community has produced. The selected contributions for the anthologies have been sourced from the extensive student archive of the V&A/RCA course and have been selected on the grounds of their quality and innovative academic content. Each volume has been edited by prominent scholars associated with the course, and through its introductory essay and range of case studies aims to provide a variety of themed approaches to the historical study of objects as powerful mediators of design, production and consumption in significant fields of material and popular culture including interior design, popular entertainment and the magazine. These anthologies are a vivid demonstration of the maturing of a discipline and offer a unique insight into the potential uses of design historical approaches as a means of unpacking the material nature of the past.

Christopher Breward

Acknowledgements

The editors would like to thank all staff and students on the RCA/V&A History of Design course who have contributed to the stimulating academic context in which much of the research toward this publication was developed. We would particularly like to thank Jeremy Aynsley, Penny Sparke, Susie McKellar, Kate Forde, Natalie Brooks, Wilhelmina Bunn and the Research Committee of the Royal College of Art, as well as Series Editor Christopher Breward, and Alison Welsby, Emma Brennan and the staff at Manchester University Press.

Introduction

Emily King and Christopher Frayling

I N T H E 1960 F I L M *The Rebel,* the central character, a city clerk-cum-aspiring artist, was played by British comedian Tony Hancock. Already a well-loved figure, Hancock endowed his character with not only his familiar radio and screen manner but also his name. This blurring of the boundary between character Tony Hancock and actor Tony Hancock is revealing of the nature of the film's design. Rather than a full-fledged cinematic setting, it is a collection of props each destined for a part in a Hancockian gag. In chapter 7 in this book, Alistair O'Neill describes the provenance of some of these props, namely a set of paintings that were cast as the work of Hancock and his fellow fictional artist Paul Ashbee. Created by Royal College of Art graduate and tutor Alistair Grant, these objects have an extremely ambiguous status. Their appearance in the film seemed to discount them as 'real' paintings, yet they were painted by an artist and in some instances had even been exhibited. It was as if fiction had trumped reality.

As a starting point to his discussion O'Neill cites a letter on *The Guardian* newspaper's Notes and Queries pages asking after the whereabouts of Hancock's supposed paintings. It seems that over time Grant's artworks have acquired a new position, cherished not for their painterly qualities but their place in popular culture. O'Neill deftly negotiates this turn of events alongside the origins of the paintings, their use in the film and their relationship to the culture of the late 1950s, both high and low. What he cannot do is definitively pin down their meaning as objects, and nor should he. To be successful, the study of entertainment design must cherish meanings in the plural.

The case of *The Rebel* is unusual, but it does demonstrate an issue that underlies all the chapters in this book: the ambiguity of the object of entertainment. It is essential that all the writers recognise their subject's dual existence as a thing and an image. Even in apparently clear-cut cases, for example David Attwood's chapter 4 study of post-war radio design 'Worlds in a Box', there is a degree of instability. Stolid as it might seem, a 1950s radio only becomes truly itself as the dispenser of a constant stream of sound. The radio's appearance is constantly inflected by its transmissions.

The gap between 'real' design and entertainment design puts the chapters in this volume in an unusual perspective vis-à-vis mainstream British design history. In a glance through the contents of the last ten years of the *Journal of Design History*, the main themes that emerge are domesticity, identity and the impact of industrial and technological change. Although the study of entertainment design does bear on all these strands, the *Journal* carries very few discussions dealing with popular imagery and popular culture. It is as if the study of design for theatre, film or TV is seen as secondary to the main event. Many of the writers in this volume have experienced this relative neglect first hand. On starting his research, Nicolas P. Maffei, author of chapter 2 'Transforming the Audience: Theatricality in the Designs of Norman Bel Geddes, 1914–19', found that the celebrated designer's work for theatre had been virtually ignored until that point. Staying with the subject, Maffei chose to disregard the standard implication that creating a stage set is less important than, for example, designing a train.

The reasons for design history's marginalisation of entertainment, popular culture and non-permanent design seem to lie in the roots of the subject. Originally a splinter group from the modernist, morally driven school of architectural history, design history has always been concerned with ideas about function and use.[1] Obviously these notions need to be radically redefined in relation to the design of entertainment. More recently, design historians have become interested in consumption and the symbolic role of designed objects,[2] but even in this expanded field the emphasis has remained on the relationship between people and things rather than the less concrete area of representation.[3]

Among the pioneers of writing about representation was the architectural-cum-design historian Reyner Banham. Alongside more conventional architectural criticism, his collection of essays *A Critic Writes* encompasses pieces on ice cream vans and the Star Wars series of films.[4] However, Banham's lead was taken up more within cultural studies than within design history.[5] As much as from architectural history and mainstream design history, the study of design for theatre, cinema and TV draws from cultural studies and related disciplines including the analysis of film. It combines enquiries about design with those about imagery, narrative, performance and culture.[6] Where design history has always been a hybrid subject, the design history of entertainment extends that mix even further.

One of the distinguishing features of historians working in this field is their relationship with collectors of ephemera and fans of popular culture. The materials of theatre, film and TV history are often preserved and ordered by enthusiasts or popularisers and this has made a great – largely unsung – contribution to the academic study of these subjects. This is most striking in the field of cinema. Rare films, posters and historical props are less likely to be found in museums than in the hands of knowledgeable individuals.[7] Referring back to the questions of the real and the fictional that bear on Alistair Grant's paintings for *The Rebel*, it seems that an appearance on screen cancels out the quality of objecthood and renders a thing uncollectable. It demotes the object. For the most part, archives of popular culture are being stored by fans. Information about them can be found, often painstakingly catalogued, on the Internet, allowing historians of film and popular music to tap into a vast and hugely informative resource from their desktops. Where many design historians scorn the 'coffee-table' or 'lifestyle' approaches, those engaged with popular culture embrace the contribution of the non-specialist audience.

Of course the argument that this book represents a break from mainstream design history is to some extent belied by its origins in the heart of the design historical establishment. It is written by nine historians, all of them at some point staff or students on the joint Royal College of Art/Victoria & Albert Museum History of Design Postgraduate course. As participants in that course, the contributors share an ambition to explore design in cultural, social, political and economic contexts. They adhere to the central tenets of the course, which include maintaining a clear view of the designed object, while avoiding the trap of vapid formalism. They explore the relationship between the object and its maker, but are not primarily concerned with questions of attribution. All the contributors are passionate about their subjects without falling back on obscure connoisseurship.

The chapters of this book have been ordered according to the nature of their subject. The contributions in the first section deal with the objects of entertainment, in other words the hardware through which images, sound and performance are transmitted. Starting with domestic hardware, the section opens with Beth Hannant's discussion in chapter 1 of theatrical lighting 'From Gas to Electric Lighting in London Theatres of the Late Nineteenth Century', followed by Nicolas Maffei's chapter 2 on Norman Bel Geddes. It continues with Josephine Kane's chapter 3 exploration of early twentieth-century cinemas in 'The construction of a modern pleasure palace: Dreamland Cinema, Margate, 1935' and ends with David Attwood's chapter 4 study of the radio set.

The second section explores the construction of cinematic and televisual imagery and the design of objects for the screen – what might be called the software of entertainment. Starting with discussions of the cinema, this section opens with Christopher Frayling in chapter 5 exploring the image of the designer in popular film 'Design and the dream factory in Britain' and moves on to Emily King's chapter 6 study of film-title sequences 'Taking credit: Saul Bass, Otto Preminger and Alfred Hitchcock' and O'Neill's chapter 7 on *The Rebel.* The latter part of the section is devoted to television, consisting of Michelle Jones's 'Design in the Monochrome Box: the BBC Television Design Department and the Modern Style, 1946–1962' as chapter 8, and then Alice Twemlow's chapter 9 on 'The Evolution of a New Televisual Language: the Sets, Title Sequences and Consumers of Ready Steady Go! 1963–66'. The book's emphasis on the 1950s and 1960s reflects the profound changes in modes of entertainment that took place during that period – in particular the spread of television, which not only attracted a huge popular audience but also prompted all other forms of entertainment to adapt. A similar shift took place during the last years of the twentieth century, when mass Internet access led to dramatic changes in existing entertainment media.

Notwithstanding this division between hardware and software, several themes are evident across the book. One of the most important of these, indeed one of the key themes of design history as a whole, is that of modernity. Among the design historian's basic texts is Marshall Berman's *All That Is Solid Melts into Air*, a book that defines modernity as the experience of living through the perpetual transformations implied by modernisation.[8] For Berman, modernity is a highly contradictory state, involving the application of a belief in progress to the lived experience of incessant change. His primary preoccupation is with literary modernism, but his ideas are applicable to many fields. Other accounts of modernism tend more toward the empirical than the philosophical. For example, in *Objects of Desire* architectural historian Adrian Forty allies the notion of modernity with that of consumer culture, a culture he traces back to the late eighteenth century.[9]

Reflecting the range of this discussion, the readings of modernity in this book are complex and multiple. Among various elements, they include a belief in a better way of life, explored here through the cinematic and televisual promotion of progress. For example Christopher Frayling's chapter relates the on-screen representation of the designer to off-screen attitudes toward the changing character of the design profession. At a more down-to-earth level, Michelle Jones's discussion of design for television illustrates the Reithian conviction that broadcasting must be used to foster social change.[10] Among her examples is the fate of *The Grove Family*, a mid-1950s TV soap opera whose characters were made to endure a fire in order that their home might be refurnished in a contemporary style. Unfortunately audiences did not accept the BBC Design Department's vision of interior design and the series was pulled from the schedules three weeks after the change in décor.

The discussion of modernity also involves tracing progressive ideas through time and across continents. In particular, it involves mapping the legacy of the German émigrés, artists and designers such as Lazslo Moholy-Nagy and Walter Gropius, who came to Britain and America to escape the Nazis. The effect of these individuals was widespread and long-lasting.[11] They worked in architecture, product design, set design, graphic design and photography and their influence bears on nearly every chapter in this book. Exploring the subject through graphics for film, Emily King's chapter 6 recounts the relationship between early twentieth-century European Modernism and its mid-century American counterpart. While pioneering Modernism was unfixed, experimental and inflected by left-wing politics, its American incarnation was emphatic, much more uniform in aesthetic and driven by the concerns of business. Articulated by Thomas Watson Jr of IBM, the slogan of US Modernism was 'good design is good business'.[12]

Although the modern project promoted by European émigrés was overwhelmingly practical in intent, its effects were often most strongly experienced in the realms of fantasy. As Josephine Kane recounts in chapter 3, the visitors strolling into Margate's Dreamland Cinema were not viewing Modernism as a means of social reform, but rather as a form of escapism. The clean architectural lines they enjoyed in cinemas were probably all the better for having no bearing on their domestic realities. In a similar vein, Frayling in chapter 5 describes audiences having little truck with the Modernist views of progress that they were shown on screen in films such as H.G. Wells's *Things to Come* (William Cameron Menzies, 1936).

Beyond these well-known characterisations of Modernism, there are other visions of progress, many of them eclectic to say the least. Geddes was a designer who flirted with the wilder fringes of modernity and his influences are described by Nicolas P. Maffei as 'Theosophy, Christian Science, advertising theory, psychology and socialism'. In keeping with his beliefs, the designer sought to move theatre audiences both emotionally and spiritually using dynamic architecture, rhythmic lighting and colour. At the heart of his vision was the notion of 'pure drama', the goal of commanding audience attention through abstract, non-narrative means. Later in the twentieth century, Geddes-style spiritualism gave way to the playfulness and immediacy of pop. Alice Twemlow's chapter 9 depiction of the pacey abstract title sequences of the popular music TV show *Ready, Steady, Go!* resonates with the idea of 'pure drama', but where Geddes hoped to take audiences to a new plane, *RSG!* was driven by nothing more profound than the need to connect with a young, increasingly media-savvy audience.

Alongside modernity, the second major theme of this book is technological change. As another of the central strands of design history, this subject is often discussed in terms of its contribution to wider developments. Where determinists (i.e., those who believe that technology dictates the nature of change) emphasise the causal role of technology, their opponents insist that culture exerts a more significant influence on our various modes of existence.[13] Orthodox technological determinism is now extremely unfashionable, but few would deny that the inventions of the nineteenth and twentieth centuries have altered the way we live. In her chapter 1, about theatre lighting, Beth Hannant points out that changes in the manner of illumination of the stage and auditorium shifted the relationship between the audience and the drama, effectively giving birth to contemporary theatrical practice. We take it for granted that theatre lighting will illuminate the actors while obscuring the audience, but in the sociable auditoria of the mid-nineteenth century this was far from the case.

According to David Attwood in chapter 4, technological developments also influenced the design of radio sets, in particular allowing the development of portable sets and encouraging the view that radios were personal rather than family possessions. Beyond questions of scale, however, the appearance of the radios was most strongly determined by fashion. Attwood describes leatherette finishes, ivory keys and an expensive set that 'looked like a minute attaché case'. Rather than technology, it appears that gender was the chief determinant of the design of radios in the 1950s. Even portable sets were viewed largely as domestic objects and, as such, women's taste usually held sway.

In parallel with these big themes, there are several other strands that run through the book. For example, both Michelle Jones and Alice Twemlow in their chapters 8 and 9 write about notions of authorised good taste in relation to the television design of the post-war period. The sense that TV should communicate something of worth to mass audiences was very strong in the early years of the medium, and remains an issue today. This discussion bears on ideas of high and low culture that are also picked out in several of the chapters. In *After the Great Divide*, cultural historian Andreas Huyssen argues that the boundary between high and low is subject to leakage and blurring.[14] Emily King develops this idea in chapter 6 with reference to the adoption of the motifs of modern art by North American graphic designers and film-makers. Once translated into popular culture, these forms achieved much wider currency, but this came at the expense of substantial alterations in meaning. In a similar vein in chapter 7, Alistair O'Neill addresses the relationship between art and film, but this time in a British context. One difference between King's and O'Neill's discussion is the British emphasis on class: in the United Kingdom high culture was, and still is, the butt of humour that sells itself as common-sense working-class. The central joke of *The Rebel* depends on the audience's perception of Tony Hancock's humble origins.

The interdependence between fantasy and reality is an enduring theme of all discussions of entertainment. A surprising characteristic of the literature thus far, has been the scant attention paid to representations of the designer in film. While film sets and costumes have been written about, respectively, by Donald Albrecht and Deborah Nadoolman Landis, Christopher Frayling's contribution to this volume in chapter 5 is to explore a new dimension: that of the image of the designer in British cinema since the 1930s.[15] He traces the story from the missionary Modernist, designer of cities of the future, to the design-engineer of wartime and Cold War Britain. This image, he suggests, gave way to the designer as gadget-maker in the 1960s' Bond movies and eventually became the urban nomad of post-industrial dereliction.

As the chapters in this book demonstrate, the relationship between design and entertainment has changed a great deal since the late nineteenth century. This change is ongoing: the nature of the spectacle is contingent on the way we lead the rest of our lives, and its evolution must be constant. This is a point made very effectively by A.P. Mohun in the article 'Designed for Thrills and Safety: Amusement Parks and the Commodification of Risk, 1880–1929'. Discussing the development of fairground rides; Mohun concludes that the market value of risk depends on the consumers' perception of day-to-day danger.[16] Almost certainly today's fairground visitors are prepared to put up with a much higher level of risk on the roads to and from the fairground than on the rides themselves.[17]

Given their range, it is no surprise that the discussions in this book draw from an extremely wide selection of literature. As well as mainstream design history, they cite specialist histories of film, television and graphic design. Recent publications in these fields include Nicholas Van Hoogstraten's *Lost Broadway Theatres*, a book that is largely nostalgic in intent, but has merits as a pictorial record.[18] Similarly, Richard Gray's *Cinemas in Britain* is an extensive visual document of the development of cinematic architecture as it moved full circle from the rectangular projection rooms of the early twentieth century through the movie-palace years, and then back to the confined spaces of the multiplex.[19] More theoretical examinations of the architecture of entertainment include that of Adnan Morshed titled 'The Aviator's (Re)Vision of the World: An Aesthetics of Ascension in Norman Bel Geddes's Futurama'[20] Morshed argues that the aerial perspective offered to visitors of the 1939 New York World Fair encouraged those spectators to form the vision of an all-seeing, all-knowing future self.

In the area of film design, several historians have questioned the assumption that sets and costumes function purely in the service of narrative. In *Pretty Pictures: Production Design and the History of Film*, the film-maker and historian C.S. Tashiro argues for a narrative-independent view of film design.[21] In defence of his perspective, Tashiro refers us to our own filmic memories, insisting that 'stories fade, images remain'.[22] Stella Bruzzi takes a related view of costume in *Undressing Cinema: Clothing and Identity in the Movies*.[23] The premise of the book is that 'clothing exists as a discourse not wholly dependent on the structures of narrative and character for signification.'[24] Bruzzi's argument focuses on the construction of gender through clothing.

Meanwhile historian Anne Massey has a different take on design for film. The main thrust of her book *Hollywood Beyond the Screen: Design and Material Culture (Materializing Culture)* is that movies have had a profound influence on real life.[25] The book emphasises the value of the 'consumer' view, drawing from Massey's own experience as a film-goer. Running along similar lines, books about TV design also tend to appeal to the reader's encounters as audience members and even as fans. Recent publications in this area include Piers D. Britton and Simon J. Barker's *Reading between Designs: Visual Imagery and the Generation of Meaning in The Avengers, The Prisoner and Doctor Who*.[26] Taking their case studies from the cult end of British TV, leaving no doubts as to their preferred viewing material, Britton and Barker propose design as a vehicle for ideas, insisting on the unity of style and content.

Film and TV graphics are usually treated in a different way. There are numerous contemporary motion-graphics compilations, mostly aimed at designers, such as *Pause: 59 Minutes of Motion Graphics*.[27] More historical accounts are rare, but include a short monograph on Kyle

Cooper with an essay by Andrea Codrington.[28] Moving away from motion graphics in particular to graphic design in general, Jeremy Aynsley's *Graphic Design in Germany, 1890–1945* has made an important contribution to the culturally and politically informed analysis of graphic design.[29] Similarly Rick Poynor's *Typographica*, the history of the design magazine of the same name that was published between 1949 and 1967, is an object lesson in locating graphic form in a particular time and place.[30]

As a meeting-point of so many different disciplines, this book can take its place in the expanding and unbordered library of the design historian specialising in entertainment. Its essays are based on detailed research from primary sources, but that does not in any way reduce the relevance to the broader field of study. Through their emphasis on detail, the authors in the book arrive at a series of conclusions that have implications for design history as a whole. It is time for design history to take more notice of popular imagery, of the ways in which design ideas are disseminated and received (as distinct from consumed). The message may sometimes be distorted in the process but that does not make it any the less important. The message may also change over time. Today's art students are likely to applaud the 'naive' paintings of Tony Hancock more than the Cézannist paintings of Paul Ashbee, which rather alters the joke.

Notes

1 For discussion of the origins of the subject see J.A. Walker and J. Attfield, *Design History and the History of Design* (London: Pluto, 1989).

2 The starting point for this kind of investigation remains Roland Barthes's key text *Mythologies*, first published in French in 1957 and translated into English in 1972 (London: Jonathan Cape, 1972).

3 The first histories of consumption tended to focus on the role of women in acquiring and lending meaning to designed objects. Among the most successful of these studies is P. Sparke, *As Long As Its Pink: The Sexual Politics of Taste* (London: Pandora, 1995). More recently interdisciplinary studies of consumption have explored the role of buying in the formation of identity across genders and social groups, for example S. Zukin and J. Smith Maguire, 'Consumers and Consumption', *Annual Review of Sociology* 30, 2004.

4   M. Banham, P. Barker, S. Lyall and C. Price (eds), *A Critic Writes: Selected Essays by Reyner Banham* (Los Angeles: University of California Press, 1997).

5   Publications on issues around representation include M. Nava, A. Blake, I. MacRury and B. Richards (eds), *Buy this Book: Studies in Advertising and Consumption* (London: Routledge, 1997). Emerging from the Centre for Consumer and Advertising Studies based in the Cultural Studies Department of the University of East London, this book contains essays on Benetton's controversial advertising campaigns and the international variations of the publication *Elle Décor*.

6   The cultural historian Dick Hebdige is a key figure in interdisciplinary studies of this sort. The chapters of the compilation *Hiding in the Light* (London: Routledge, 1988) are exemplary studies of the objects of popular taste in the wider cultural context.

7   In Britain the two best collections of posters and stills are the John Kobal Collection and the Ronald Grant Collection. In France, the collection of Henri Langlois was so extensive that it became a museum in its own right.

8   M. Berman, *All That Is Solid Melts Into Air: The Experience of Modernity* (New York: Simon and Schuster, 1982).

9   A. Forty, *Objects of Desire: Design and Society, 1750–1980* (London: Thames & Hudson, 1986).

10 John Reith was the founding Director General of the British Broadcasting Corporation, holding the post between 1922 and 1938. His insistence on the educational and cultural responsibilities of public-service broadcasting remains influential.

11 For an account of the influence of many of these émigrés see S. Barron with S. Eckmann, the 1997 Los Angeles County Museum of Art catalogue *Exiles + Émigrés: The Flight of European Artists from Hitler* (New York: N. Abrams, 1997).

12 S. Heller, *Paul Rand* (London: Phaidon, 1999), p. 145.

13 Among the most important texts on the influence of technology is S. Giedion, *Mechanization Takes Command* (New York: W.W. Norton, 1969). Writing in the mid-1940s, Giedion believed that mechanisation operates as an independent force with the power to overcome humanity. Since then, this view has been challenged by historians such as J. Wajcman, *Feminism Confronts Technology* (Philadelphia, PA: Pennsylvania State University Press, 1991). Where Giedion characterises mechanisation as a free-standing element, Wajcman emphasises its cultural roots.

14 A. Huyssen, *After the Great Divide: Modernism, Mass Culture and Post-Modernism* (Bloomington, IN: Indiana University Press, 1986).

15 D. Albrecht, *Designing Dreams: Modern Architecture in the Movies* (London: Thames & Hudson, 1987). D.N. Landis, *Dressed: A Century of Hollywood Costume Design* (New York: Collins Design, 2007).

16 A.P. Mohun, 'Designed for Thrills and Safety: Amusement Parks and the Commodification of Risk, 1880–1929', *Journal of Design History* 14(4), 2001, pp. 291–306.

17 For further discussion of the contingent nature of the spectacle and entertainment as a category see R. Dyer, *Only Entertainment* (London: Routledge, 2002). Exploring whether an emphasis on pleasure is the defining quality of entertainment (vis-à-vis other forms of art), Dyer unpicks the historical and cultural construction of the term.

18 N. Van Hoogstraten, *Lost Broadway Theatres* (New York: Princeton Architectural Press, 1997).

19 R. Gray, *Cinemas in Britain* (London: Lund Humphries, 1996).

20 Unpublished thesis by A. Morshed, 'The Aviator's (Re)Vision of the World: An Aesthetics of Ascension in Norman Bel Geddes's Futurama' (Boston, MA: Massachusetts Institute of Technology, 2001).

21 C.S. Tashiro, *Pretty Pictures: Production Design and the History of Film* (Austin, TX: University of Texas Press, 1998).

22 Ibid., p. 59.

23 S. Bruzzi, *Undressing Cinema: Clothing and Identity in the Movies* (London: Routledge, 1998).

24 Ibid., p. xvi.

25 A. Massey, *Hollywood Beyond the Screen: Design and Material Culture (Materializing Culture)* (Oxford: Berg, 2000).

26 P.D. Britton and S.J. Barker, *Reading between Designs: Visual Imagery and the Generation of Meaning in The Avengers, The Prisoner and Doctor Who* (Austin, TX: University of Texas Press, 2003).

27 P. Hall, A. Codrington, J. Hirschfeld and S. Barth, *Pause: 59 Minutes of Motion Graphics* (New York: Universe Books, 2000).

28 A. Codrington, *Kyle Cooper* (London: Laurence King, 2003).

29 J. Aynsley, *Graphic Design in Germany, 1890–1945* (London: Thames & Hudson, 2000).

30 R. Poynor, *Typographica* (London: Laurence King, 2001).

I
DESIGN AND POPULAR ENTERTAINMENT: HARDWARE

1 ✧ From gas to electric lighting in London theatres of the late nineteenth century

Beth Hannant

Introduction

This chapter examines the introduction of electricity to London's theatres from the end of the nineteenth century. It traces the early electrical experiments that were carried out in the theatre and analyses the impact of the new technology on both interior and stage design, with the resulting implications this held for the audience. Finally it questions why this arena in particular was first chosen for the introduction of electricity.

The development of an electrical power supply and the invention of the electric arc and the incandescent lamp were the major technological advances behind the transformation of theatre lighting during the 1880s. Before 1885, prior to electrification, the set and the auditorium were not treated as separate spaces for the purposes of lighting, but by the end of this period, newer lighting systems created a division between the audience and the stage, the performance and its reception. This resulted in an entirely new experience of theatre, and it was one driven as much by technical possibilities as by artistic or aesthetic concerns.

Looking more closely at this transition, four significant lighting events that took place at popular theatre venues located along the Strand demonstrate the changes in the application of technology to theatre design, and also changes in the consumption of theatre by the public. With particular reference to the Gaiety, the Savoy and the Lyceum, I will illustrate how lighting helped directors reformulate the sense of stage lighting and interior space, ultimately breaking from the tradition of a unified lighting scheme to one which emphasised the division between stage and auditorium.

This study is not without its methodological difficulties. For instance, a recent theatre design exhibition foregrounded a problem frequently encountered when examining lighting and performance: 'lighting is still the most elusive of theatrical arts to capture, quantify and exhibit. Because it is a combination of so many elements in real space and time of performance it cannot be separated from a live performance.'[1] It is easy to lose the crucial role of lighting in the interaction within a scene, and the transition from one scene to another. Beyond this, the 'in-house' information regarding actual performances is limited mostly to promotional material. Therefore, this discussion makes consistent use of newspaper reviews and contemporary accounts of events, in order to recreate both an image of these theatre interiors and a sense of how they were experienced by the Victorian public.[2]

Lighting technologies

Electric lighting in Britain did not completely replace older technologies for some decades; and from its introduction in the 1880s until many years after the period of this study, electric light had to prove its superiority to a number of competing sources: Gas, Limelight, Carbon Light, The Incandescent Lamp and Electrical supply.[3]

Prior to electrification, natural gas was the main source of theatrical lighting, which had in turn superseded candlelight and the oil-argand burner at the start of the nineteenth century.[4] One example of a gas lighting system was that used at the New Strand theatre in 1832. Footlights at the front of the stage had polished and reflective brass flame- or leaf-shaped guards to maximise the emission of light; chandeliers hung from the balconies with glass prisms reflecting into the auditorium; and battens were used in the wings and above the stage to create an overall floodlighting effect. In many ways, however, the distribution of light through the interior using gas technology had not progressed far beyond the results achieved with candles and oil.

It was not until the introduction of a competitor, the electric incandescent lamp, that gas manufacturers started experimenting with special effects using screens, scrims and combinations of steam and chemical pyrotechnics to create coloured lighting effects upon the stage. Gas was supplied in bags and the only means of creating different lighting states was if they were jumped on backstage, giving a stronger light for an actor's entrance.[5] Up until the early twentieth century, gas continued to be used while electric lighting technologies were in their early stages of development. The Welsbach mantel, for example, was invented in 1885, seven years after the invention of the electric incandescent lamp. It contained the gas flame within a glass frame, thus increasing the light output threefold, and was developed for use in public spaces. In addition to being spurred on by the competition (and even the candle industry developed new ways of mass producing greater quantities at cheaper prices), newer gas lighting inventions were also influenced by electrical developments. The Welsbach mantel was adapted directly from the incandescent lamp's glass globe that created and protected the light source.

Limelight, which had been invented in 1820 for the purpose of surveying at night, was in widespread use for theatre lighting during the late nineteenth century. Created by a block of compressed quicklime heated to incandescence by a naked coal-gas flame, it was the only source capable of producing a projection, and gave off a green light mainly used for floodlighting. Its main disadvantage was that it required constant attention by its operator, and was highly dangerous around flammable scenery. Limelight jets, lenses, gasbags and other apparatus were still being advertised in trade magazines in the 1880s.[6] However, by the 1890s limelight suppliers had begun to advertise electrical goods alongside their traditional paraphernalia.

The first attempt to replace theatre lighting with electricity was demonstrated in 1802, using the carbon arc light, but was not viable for public use for several decades. It was constructed from two metallic carbon rods connected in series with a resistance for limiting the current in an electrical circuit; when the rods touched, the carbons combusted, emitting a powerful light. It, too, needed constant supervision because it was hand-held and difficult to manage, and gave off burning sparks of carbon. Although carbon arc light provided an early form of spotlighting, this method still produced a flicker and was not suitable for interiors.

These alternative technologies competed fiercely for the

predominance of the national light source, but why was there a delay in
the prevalent use of an electrical light source in Britain? Electric interior
lighting was not feasible until the development of the incandescent
lamp. This source of light energy, emanating from a carbon filament
within a vacuum-sealed bottle, was invented simultaneously by Joseph
Swan in Great Britain and Thomas Edison in the United States in 1879.
Although it is possible to see developments in electrical technology
occurring throughout the nineteenth century, the main requirement
for its widespread use came with the supply of electricity for lighting
uses. In these early years, the issues deciding the electrification of
London were installation, cost and reliable supply. However, there were
complicating factors. In the words of G. Basil-Bartham, author of *The
Development of the Incandescent Lamp*, there appeared to be 'no evidence
of public resistance ... the biggest resistance came from special groups
with vested interests'.[7] The groups to which he was referring were local
councils and gas companies, who had their own plans for positioning gas
as the main power supply by working to ensure an efficient and regular
supply and developing their own lamp designs.[8] Gas itself was being
mixed to produce a better cleaner light (and with less air pollution) and
was still seen in these quarters as a developing technology.[9] Electricity,
after all, was expensive, its high price determined in part by the small
quantities being generated and used. And in consequence, London was
slow in establishing a central supply.[10] Moreover, the responsibility
for setting up any sort of supply fell to local authorities, which were
hesitant about committing their resources to electricity, expressing
a reluctance to invest in the necessary experimentation. The fight to
standardise the supply was further hindered by undecided boroughs
unwilling to commit themselves.[11]

The advantages of electricity were clearer to the municipal
authorities in Paris. A Parisian report from 1878 detailed a number
of the advantages of instantaneous light, including the saving of time
and labour involved in extinguishing gas flames.[12] The report went
on to state that this 'vastly superior light' smelt better, was brighter
and 'caused no accidents to horses, through blindness', an obvious
concern. Even so, despite its benefits, electricity was rejected as a
suitable light source for street lighting, and was only seen in Britain to
be practical in creating one-off 'splendid effects in large squares'.[13] It is

possible that this report and others like it offered those in the theatre the opportunity to engage in this debate by rising to the challenge of lighting large public spaces.

The following four lighting events demonstrate the role of theatre within these debates and assess the specific contribution of electricity to the design of theatrical lighting.

The Gaiety Theatre, 1878

Surprisingly this important technology was not at first applied to the stage, as one might have expected, but to the theatre's exterior. The first instance of this in London occurred at The Gaiety Theatre in 1878. The Gaiety was the first theatre in England to use electric light, using arc light, an initiative that the theatre took in direct response to the Parisian report. Having taken the advice of a 'French scientific gentleman', the theatre manager went ahead with his electrical display, 'which I am burning every night in the Strand'.[14] His experimentation proved that, if electric light replaced gas, it could produce twenty times the illumination at only five times the cost. By reducing the number of lamps, and making other improvements, the cost difference between gas and electricity would be equalised. The only reference to the visual aspect of the display is to be found in a contemporary theatre journal that described 'The Gaiety illuminated so brilliantly by electric light'.[15] This and other discussions in electrical journals reveal that it was the technological feat of applying electricity to the exterior of the Gaiety that caused a sensation, rather than the visual effect itself. The design of striking electrical lighting effects was to be developed later.

London's theatreland venues still resemble these Victorian theatres today, where the shells have been preserved for over a hundred years. With the establishment of electricity the number of annual theatre fires dropped. Therefore, like a stopped watch these buildings reveal the last moment in time at which they were socially significant, playing an important role in attracting the public through impressive theatrical spectacles. For instance, the rotating ball on top of the London Coliseum which dates from 1906 and is recreated with lighting today, is a testament to the safety of electricity, considering that so many of the gas-lit theatres had repeatedly burnt to the ground.[16]

The Savoy Theatre, 1881

Not only was the Savoy the first theatre to use electric incandescent lamps to illuminate its front of house, auditorium, dressing rooms and stage, it also represented the first ever attempt to light any public building entirely with electricity. Once again, however, the lighting design for the stage could not be separated from the experience of lighting in other parts of the theatre. The Savoy experiment of 1881 was used in a production of *Patience* by Gilbert and Sullivan under the management of Richard D'Oyly Carte. *Patience* was already a favourite opera at the time and had gained a following during its successful touring in Britain and the United States. The Savoy's choice of the play is significant, therefore, as it gave the audience a sense of the production both before and after electrification.

The Savoy used the new electric incandescent lamp manufactured by Swan of Newcastle, and the Siemen brothers supplied the generator apparatus. There were a total of 1,200 lamps, and the large steam engines, producing 120 horsepower, had to be positioned on a nearby patch of open land. The project encountered a number of obstacles, the most prominent being the need to produce enough energy to supply the entire building, and prevent any loss of electrical supply during the performance. Further generating apparatus had to be brought in; along with an emergency gas supply to light the auditorium in seconds should the electrical method fail. Indeed the play's name became unintentionally apt when technical problems delayed the opening night by a week. Once it did open, only the front of house and auditorium were lit; it took another two months to refine the lighting systems sufficiently to light the stage. Only then was gaslight completely abandoned. This project highlights the difficulties involved in transferring to a new power supply, particularly since the theatre itself had not been built to accommodate the design requirements of the new technology. The Savoy was later renovated to accommodate the generators, and D'Oyly Carte's later theatres incorporated these improvements from the outset.[17] For some time before the opening night D'Oyly Carte wrote of *Patience* for *The Times* and a range of theatrical newspapers, reporting on the progress of the conversion to electricity. In so doing, he astutely created a groundswell of excitement surrounding the event. In this way, potential audiences were invited to take part in the progress of the experiment inside and outside the theatre. The articles were careful to stress the safety of the new product. One advertisement in particular in the *Daily News* claimed that

> A herd of wild buffaloes suddenly turned loose among the intricate details of the woodland scene of the second act, of PATIENCE, might trample down 'groundrows' and sweep away, and destroy whole 'battens' and hanging 'winglights', scattering literally hundreds of lamps among the wreck of inflammable canvas and frail woodwork, but assuredly they could not set fire to the Savoy stage while lighted only by this means.[18]

The conversion to electricity was not the only measure boasted at the Savoy for the health and safety of the audience. The exits and entrances were increased so that the audience could be cleared in three minutes, and new fire-resisting materials were being employed on the stage and in the passages and stairways.[19] The Savoy was the first theatre to be built under an 1878 act of parliament that was particularly stringent toward fire prevention; and this may have been closely involved with D'Oyly Carte's decision to trust in the future of electricity. Due to growing public awareness of their own health and welfare and the enforcement of these new fire and safety regulations, changes to the interiors of public buildings were inevitable. The Savoy was also unique in being the first theatre to implement new ways of controlling the public's use of its interiors. Seating plans were carefully designed so that the audience was given a clear view of the stage from every seat, and everyone was allocated a specific seat with his or her purchase of a ticket. This had not been the case in theatres until this time, and replaced the music-hall system of 'first come first seated', which had caused overcrowding and great fire hazards. This promoted the introduction of differentiated seating prices and as a result was used to separate different social classes among the clientele. Therefore, according to contemporary opinion, theatres became more civilised and respectable environments – a notion to which the 'aesthetic operas' of Gilbert and Sullivan were clearly aspiring. It was a concern for the theatre to define itself against rowdy, drunken music-hall entertainment, which was achieved through its use of lighting and design. On another point, Richard D'Oyly Carte claimed that

> if the experiment of electric lighting succeeds, there can be no question of the enormous advantages to be gained in the purity of air and coolness – advantages to which it is hardly possible to over estimate … I venture to think that the interiors of most theatres hitherto built have been conceived with little, if any artistic purpose, and generally executed with little completeness, and in a more or less garish manner.[20]

With electricity in place, interiors could employ lighting for visual and decorative effects of a different order from the bold and garish decoration that had been used before. With gas lighting, theatre interiors needed redecorating every year due to the soot and fumes. By contrast, the Savoy went eight years before redecorating after its conversion to electricity. The point was not lost on the *Leeds Mercury*, who, in March 1894, turned to the Savoy as a shining example of a better alternative to gas.[21] When the audience entered the theatre in October 1881, the cast sang the national anthem and D'Oyly Carte delivered a speech on the 'experiment'. When the main gaslights were finally lowered, a contemporary report in *The Times* described how

> all eyes were turned towards the pear-shaped lamps beneath the centre of the gallery, the upper circle, and the balcony tiers. As if by a wave of a fairy's wand the theatre immediately became filled with a soft, soothing light, clearer and more grateful than gas.[22]

There were reports of occasional flickers during the first performances due to the experimental nature of the equipment. One audience member was concerned that the white pear-shaped lamps should be replaced by yellow ones because they gave off 'too much light' (in reality they only emitted the equivalent of 25 watts).[23] During the interval, D'Oyly Carte took to the stage and proceeded to explain the system, and the advantages of intensity control that it offered. He also wrapped a lamp in a piece of highly flammable muslin and smashed the glass, which destroyed the vacuum and extinguished the flame instantly. The demonstrations were treated as though they were part of the entertainment and the audience were further invited to participate by examining the apparatus and lamps on stage after the performance. One cartoon caricature shows D'Oyly Carte dressed as Peter Pan holding up a lamp and electrifying the Savoy himself. As theatre manager he was seen as the entrepreneur of electrification, effectively endorsing the new product.[24]

Theatrical experimentation did not remain isolated to London. The Paris Opera House had managed that same year to light one scene using electric arc lighting. In Paris, however, the experiment was more concerned with creating an ambience on the stage, and seemed to lack the broader social and cultural agenda driving the Savoy's innovations. For D'Oyly Carte, electricity also created publicity for the relaunch of the Savoy, and the public's genuine fears of electricity were by and large assuaged. Like the Gaiety, the Savoy offered itself as an example of improved conditions and may well have had the effect of increasing public pressure on the government to take responsibility for the centralisation of electricity supply. At the same time, however, events at the Gaiety and the Savoy are more significant for their role in using theatre as a means of communicating the relevance of electric lighting than for the ground-breaking nature of their lighting designs. Although the technology was different, it was used in much the same way as gas, lamp for lamp. In some ways the publicity surrounding the application of electric light at the Savoy and the Gaiety stimulated further developments of gas lighting in other theatres.

The Lyceum Theatre, 1885

The Lyceum Theatre was the first theatre to install gas on the stage in 1817. The Lyceum was to gas lighting what the Savoy was to electric lighting: a platform for the experimentation and marketing of a new technology (see Figure 1.1). Although electric lighting was superior in terms of its visual potential, the Lyceum's artistic director and theatre manager Henry Irving did more to define stage design as a separate concern from the theatre as a whole than the Savoy ever attempted. Irving's 1885 production of *Faust* saw the first occasion in British theatre history when the house lights were dimmed and then extinguished during part of the performance.[25] This was a key moment in theatre history in that, through lighting, the stage was the main focus and

INTERIOR OF THE LYCEUM THEATRE, REDECORATED.

1.1 This interior view of the Lyceum Theatre from 1847 illustrates how the auditorium was gas lit throughout the performance and the stage lit from the front by the flames from a row of gas footlights.

separated from the audience for the purpose of dramatic effect. This production also marked Irving's direct move away from the two-dimensional backdrop *trompe l'oeil* effect, lit by footlights at the front of the stage and in the wings. New developments in gas lighting meant that he could light specific areas of the set while the others remained in darkness. This allowed him to construct a more elaborate, three-dimensional set. The set was constructed from moulded cardboard – imitating brick and stone in some scenes – and the new and more easily manipulable lighting techniques were able to create more effective shadowing, and were better at picking out specific details. This should also be seen in the context of a time in which there was a growing demand in theatres for 'historical-representation', 'naturalism' and realistic set dressing (frequently influenced by European theatre), which brought more props and clutter to the stage.[26]

The progression of specific, on-stage lighting, 1883–1900

The new potential of electric light was demonstrated at its most extreme in a device first developed in London for the Savoy's performance of *Iolanthe* in 1883.[27] Here, a particular development, patented in 1887, consisted of tiny lamps sewn into the costumes or used in the headdresses of the chorus ladies and principal performers. The lights were eventually attached to batteries carried by each actor, but before these devices included individual on-off switches controlled by the wearer, the actors were dangerously wired up directly to the theatre's electrical supply. These lights were quickly adopted in other English theatres including Manchester's Theatre Royal. Another reference to the use of such a device can be found in a production of *A Midsummer Night's Dream* on 11 June 1900, at the Majesties Theatre. One account noted how the production began

> in darkness … but soon electric lights on the head and wings of the fairies – aerial and on foot – glint through the trees … Oberon, glorious in gold, represents the sun, and the effects of cloth trappings of bullion, jewels on the corsage, pale green wings, and a sun crown on her head, are accentuated by electric light cunningly introduced into her costume.[28]

Various adaptations of these devices existed and were written about in nineteenth-century theatre literature. The strobes and rays, depicted in the Paris 1900 exhibition, also demonstrate that the French had been quick to grasp the more intricate techniques of electric lighting, while the British maintained their fascination with fairy-light-style decorative effects well into the twentieth century.[29]

In 1891 the Lyceum theatre finally gave way to the technological progression of electricity. This occurred at the same time as most of Britain's provincial theatres were taking the same leap, and consecutively with one theatre in North America. American theatres were some of the last buildings to be electrified. The benefits of electricity were more obvious and simplified within a rural, spread-out environment than to a densely populated city like London. Therefore, with little resistance to the new technology, US domestic interiors were electrified long beforehand.[30] This contrast emphasises the importance of the theatre in the development of electrical technology within Britain. Nonetheless it still took another twenty years before the electricity supply had been standardised in Britain[31] and it was forty years before the majority of private houses were connected to the grid.[32] Britain's rapid electrification of theatres is something of an anomaly.

In North America by contrast, theatres were the last buildings to be electrified and the focus was very much on introducing electricity within domestic interiors.[33] This forty-year delay in the standardisation of electrical apparatus is illustrated in the catalogues of the General Electric Company. In the 1880s, the first electric lamps were simply replacements for the flames in gas lamps and lamps were wired directly into the current where required. One lamp type serviced all industries with the bayonet and screw fittings still to be developed. It was twenty years after the invention of the incandescent lamp before specialist theatre lamps, switchboards and dimmers were introduced, as can be seen in trade catalogues from 1901. Generally speaking, contemporary electrical equipment could have been adapted for any space, but in London it was the theatre world that promoted its use before the domestic sphere. It is possible therefore that, while theatres in England played an instrumental role in familiarising their audience's with electricity, they initially maintained its reputation as an exceptional and chiefly spectacular lighting effect rather than household commodity.

Theatre and society: the Victorian preoccupation with looking

The attraction of the theatre in the nineteenth century often had very little to do with the performance and much to do with being seen at the event of the evening. Many theatres such as the Gaiety and Savoy also had restaurants, smoking rooms for the men and lounges for ladies. This is reminiscent of the music hall, in which entertainment was combined with eating and drinking (more typically the latter in the case of the music-hall).[34] The theatre was a place to meet and socialise, and this frequently overrode the attraction of the performance, as an analysis of the all-over lighting schemes will reveal. During this period box-office takings had begun to drop. Lighting experimentation and spectacle were the perfect gimmicks to boost figures and attract audiences back. At the fashionable Savoy and Lyceum theatres, first nights were for the well-heeled only. On other nights wealthy patrons occupied the pit and gallery, while the upper circles were filled with the 'humbler middle classes, students and a sprinkling of working class'.[35]

Formal dress was essential to the event, and theatre historian Michael Booth has commented that these lavishly attired 'spectators gave the theatre of the period a sense of satirical pomp and magnificence, entirely suited to the elaborate spectacle on stage'.[36] When the Savoy became electrically lit, not only did the garish decor change from heavy gilt to mellow yellows, but so did the costumes of the audience. In particular, the ladies' dress was changed from heavy cosmetics and coloured jewels to softer tones and diamonds.[37] To the theatrical reviewers of the period, descriptions of the ladies' costumes in the crowd became as important as the theatrical costumes and the stage itself.

Coming finally to the stage itself, in this period it became the fashion for the stage to be equipped with furniture, drapes and everyday objects, such as could be purchased for any private domestic interior.[38] Percy Fitzgerald's theatrical descriptions from the 1890s note that

> the most complicated and familiar objects about us are fearlessly laid hold of by the property man, and dragged upon the stage. Thus, when we take our dramatic pleasure, we have the satisfaction of not being separated from the objects of our daily life, and within the walls of the theatre we meet again the engine and train that set us down almost at the door.[39]

He goes on to explain the replacement of the property man by the antiques dealer and the involvement of the 'modish shop and the professional decorator'.[40] The director, the manager, and the scenic artists frequently shared the responsibility for stage design during the nineteenth century, and it was not until the 1920s and 1930s that set and costume designers developed as specialised posts with responsibility for stage design. As was the case with lighting, nineteenth-century theatres were as much concerned with the design and decor of the auditorium as with that of the stage (arrangement of the latter being referred to as stage decoration rather than stage design). At the Savoy, on the opening of *Patience*, the auditorium was described in terms of moods:

> Comfort and cheerfulness befitting the home of comic Opera have evidently been the guiding motives of the decorators. Sombre hues and deep-toned colours have been purposely avoided, the prevailing tints being delicate gold and white ... and the general effect is upon the whole, harmonious, although not strikingly beautiful.[41]

There are no descriptions of the stage itself. Even with conscious attempts to direct attention away from the auditorium to the stage – like the turning off of the house lights – managers were still faced with the problem that audiences had preconditioned expectations of what they should look at and how they should look at it. As the same review stubbornly continued: 'The favourable impression previously recorded was fully confirmed last night when the blaze of light on the well-dressed audience added to the brightness of the scene' (see Figure 1.2).[42] What electrical lighting often brought to theatre, therefore, was more light to see what everyone else was wearing and how the theatre manager was furnishing his theatre lounges.

From spectacle to modernity

The bond between spectacle and new technology did not instantly bring with it sophisticated apparatus for controlling lighting. It took time both to develop such equipment and for electricians to attain the necessary level of expertise. This process was also heavily reliant on the enthusiasm of amateurs, with their 'large biscuit tins ... electric bulbs and sheets of gelatine',[43] whose work in church halls and schools often proved more experimental than West End productions. The work of new playwrights demanded a re-envisioning of stage design, and lighting technology was employed as part of this effort. Playwrights subsequently began to write scenes into plays which depended on

---

1.2 *opposite* The interior of the New Savoy Theatre, 1881. Contemporary journals described how the 'pear-shaped' incandescent electric lamps gave an immediate, soft, soothing and clearer light.

THE NEW SAVOY THEATRE.

1.3 *'In the flies' at Drury Lane Theatre* by J. Swain, 1884. This illustration reveals the theatrical use of 'battens' and 'winglights'.

lighting techniques for dramatic effect, replacing the set and need for elaborate furnishings. This marked the key moment when lighting met drama and spectacle gave way to more naturalistic forms of theatre.

Strindberg claimed that with *Miss Julie*, written in 1888, he was offering the 'first naturalistic tragedy'.[44] However, it was not publicly performed until 1892 and did not reach London until 1912. He explained his frustration with sets made from canvas with painted details of rooms and called for the use of scenic materials that would eliminate 'tiresome exits' which sent the canvas flapping at the slightest touch, destroyed the illusion and distracted from the drama. He identified the need for realism in a single set, with doors that slammed and pans that clattered. His idea of theatre was to mirror life in every physical detail. More importantly, he called for the removal of the footlights and the use of strong sidelights to bring out the expressions on the actors' faces. Auditoria were to be kept in complete darkness and the orchestra kept out of sight, so nothing would distract from the stage. Where possible, auditoria and stages should be small to create a more intimate environment between actor and spectator. Strindberg's stage directions were light years from the productions of the London theatre scene. He impatiently anticipated the day when: 'a new drama might emerge and theatre might become a place for educated people. While we await such a theatre, one must write to create a stock of plays in readiness for the repertoire that will, some day, be needed.'[45] The developments in electric lighting enabled the playwright to encourage this intellectual environment with its immediate control on the prominence of stage over auditorium.

Once modern playwrights started to write with newer technologies in mind, lighting began to change the entire appearance of performances. Up until this time, lighting technology had been used to move attention onto the stage, but not to articulate the space itself. New writing and new technologies creatively influenced one another, and through this fusion stage design came to engage with modernity.

Conclusion

This chapter has explored the complex relationship of new electrical technologies with the Victorian theatre. What was new to the Victorian era was that the material culture of theatre percolated into the commercial sphere, with electric lighting acting as a technological link between these two arenas. Theatrical spectacle was used as a means of communicating ideas to the masses; a popular language understood and accepted by society, and manipulated to bring attention to new ideas. In his book 'The Commodity Culture of Victorian England: Advertising & Spectacle, 1851–1914', Thomas Richards describes how 'spectacle functioned as a kind of experimental theatre for industrial capitalism'.[46] As audiences came to expect more, the need for spectacle acquired a dynamic of its own and spiralled ever upward. This is not to say that the Savoy and Gaiety were using spectacle to create consumer demand but that their achievements were adopted by commodity-driven industries, and were then aimed at consumers. Then, with time, the 'spectacularization of the commodity',[47] to borrow Richards's phrase, entered mainstream salesmanship. As for electric lighting, a commodity in its own right, this led the way for many other electrically powered devices once electrification had become commonplace. Theatre provided an environment and an audience, and conditioned people to appreciate and anticipate spectacles. Spectacle then accelerated the demand for more commodities, feeding the cycle of shopping and consumption.

Once electric light had become generally accepted, it became intertwined with the development of theatre in the twentieth century (see Figure 1.3). As the century progressed, new waves of theatrical writing along with the rising profession of the stage design, soon took electric lighting for granted and began to exploit its potential in a range of innovative ways.

Notes

1 The Theatre Lighting Designers Society, *Time Space, Design for Performance 1995–1999*, Royal College of Art Exhibition, 2000.

2 This study proceeds from the belief that the multi-sensorial experience of Victorian theatre may be recreated through the details of historical information. This view shares some similarities with the New Historicist practice of literary theory most famously associated with the work of scholar Stephen Greenblatt in the area of Renaissance theatre studies. Greenblatt and others have challenged the traditional view of literature as an independent realm of discourse. Instead they advocate an approach to texts that pays particular attention to their historical situation, not merely as a colourful backdrop to the 'real' world, but as an integral part of it. Their work often concerns itself with the material circumstances of Renaissance drama in terms of lighting, stage design, costume, etc. New Historicist critics will use contemporary ephemera such as maps, miniatures, personal accounts or contemporary tracts to contextualise a play's ideological subtext. This kind of comparative analysis is considered to be just as relevant as any formal discussion of literary style. See for instance S.J Greenblatt, *Renaissance Self-Fashioning: From More to Shakespeare* (Chicago: University of Chicago Press, 1980); A.R. Jones and P. Stallybrass (eds), *Renaissance Clothing and the Materials of Memory* (Cambridge and New York: Cambridge University Press, 2000); J. Dollimore and A. Sinfield (eds), *Political Shakespeare: Essays in Cultural Materialism* (Manchester: Manchester University Press, 1994).

3 For a comprehensive account of the development of artificial light during this period see W. Schivelbusch's classic study *Disenchanted Night: The Industrialisation of Light in the Nineteenth Century,* trans. A. Davies (Berkeley and London: University of California Press, 1988). Schivelbusch argues that new systems of lighting technology actually changed sensibilities and helped shape modern consciousness.

4 For an assessment of the role of lighting in theatre design see G. Izenour, *Theater Technology* (New Haven and London: Yale University Press, 1996), p. 79.

5 For a complete history of theatre lighting during this period see T. Rees, *Theatre Lighting In the Age of Gas* (London: Society for Theatre Research), 1978.

6 'Dale and Crampton Manufacturers & Frederic J. Cox Manufacturer', *Era* (18 January 1880), p. 16.

7 G. Basil-Bartham, *The Development of the Incandescent Lamp* (London: Scott Greenwood & Son, 1912), p. 504.

8 'Experiments in Gas Lighting', *The Electric Light* (18 January 1879).

9 Gas systems continued to be fitted in interiors into the twentieth century. See Rees, *Theatre Lighting.*

10 T. Hughes, *Networks of Power* (London: Johns Hopkins University Press, 1993), p. 227.

11 Hackney & Shoreditch promoted the centralisation of electrical supply while other boroughs rejected the possibility. A bill of 1882 outlined local authorities' intention to encourage private experimentation 'as cheaply as possible', and after 15 years would purchase the plants at a 'reasonable price' without any risk taken. *The Electrician* (4 August 1882), p. 298.

12 See the findings of the 1878 report by Chelsea Council outlining the benefits and disadvantages of electric street lighting in Paris. *The Times* (August 1878).

13 *The Times* (August 1878).

14 In his theatre journal, Gaiety Theatre manager John Hollingshead responds to the Chelsea Council report. 'The electric light', *Era* (25 August 1878), p. 13.

15 Photographs seldom depicted scenes of lighting. *Era* (18 August 1878), p. 5.

16 Theatre fires caused by gas lighting span the nineteenth-century pages of *Era,* the weekly trade paper for the theatre and music halls.

17 D'Oyly Carte built The Royal English Opera House in 1889–91, at Cambridge circus, and it became The Palace Theatre in 1892.

18 J.D. Poulter, 'The Story of the Electrification of Leeds', *An Early History of Electrical Supply* (London: Peter Peregrinus, 1986), p. 41.

19 Advertisement for new patents increasing improvements in fireproofing feature in *Era* over the next 10 years. 'Preparation For Rendering Wood Fabrics Incombustible', *Era* (9 July 1890), Patent no. 10,589.

20 *The Times* (6 October 1881).

21 Poulter, *An Early History of Electrical Supply*, p. 122.

22 Rees, *Theatre Lighting*, p. 170.

23 Ibid., p. 171.

24 The cartoonist has inaccurately depicted an arc lamp. 'The Savoy Theatre', *D'Oyly Carte Centenary 1875–1975*.

25 M. Booth, *Victorian Spectacular Theatre* (London: Routledge & Kegan Paul, 1981), p. 95.

26 A.M. Nagler, *A Source Book in Theatrical History* (New York: Dover Publications, 1952), p. 579. As J. Richards notes in *Sir Henry Irving: A Victorian Actor and His World* (London: Hambledon and London, 2005), published to mark the centenary of Irving's death, Irving removed the electric light installed in the theatre during his absence on tour in America, and lit his productions thereafter by limelight and gaslight, which he considered created more artistic effects.

27 Rees, *Theatre Lighting*, p. 181.

28 Oberon the fairy-king appears to have been played by a woman, unless the reference to 'her' is an editorial mistake. Booth, *Victorian Spectacular Theatre*, p. 128.

29 *L'Expédition de Paris 1900*, Vols 1 and 3 (Paris: Montgredien & Cie, 1899).

30 G. Bergman, *Lighting In Theatre* (Sweden: Almquist & Wiksell International, 1977).

31 In 1900 London was the largest city in the Western world with a population of 7.25 million, yet Greater London had 65 electrical utilities, 70 generating stations, 49 different types of supply systems, 10 frequencies, 32 voltage levels for transmission and 24 for distribution and 70 methods of paying – further hindering the move toward one central supply. See Hughes, *Networks of Power*, p. 227.

32 With a central supply, consumption would increase as electrical goods became standardised, enabling their mass production. Hughes, *Networks of Power*, p. 228.

33 L. Hannah, *Electricity Before Nationalisation* (London: Macmillan, 1979), p. 182.

34 A. Hyman, *The Gaiety Years* (London: Cassell, 1975), p. 24.

35 A cross-section of society was represented across a single performance. Booth *Victorian Spectacular Theatre*, p. 95.

36 Ibid.

37 W. Von Eckardt, *Oscar Wilde's London* (London: Westminster Archive), p. 56.

38 Advertisement for household furnishings, Oetzmann & Co., *Era* (9 July 1890), p. 11.

39 Booth *Victorian Spectacular Theatre*, p. 15.

40 Ibid., p. 15.

41 'The Savoy Theatre', *The Times* (3 October 1881).

42 Ibid.

43 H. Ridge, *Stage Lighting* (Cambridge: W. Heffer & Sons Ltd., 1928), preface, unpaginated.

44 A. Strindberg, *Plays One, Miss Julie* (London: Methuen Drama, 1987), p. 85.

45 Ibid., p. 103.

46 T. Richards, *The Commodity Culture of Victorian England: Advertising and Spectacle, 1851–1914* (New York: Verso, 1990), p. 56.

47 Ibid., p. 58.

2 ✧ Transforming the audience: theatricality in the designs of Norman Bel Geddes, 1914–1939

Nicolas P. Maffei

NORMAN BEL GEDDES, 1893–1958, was one of America's most important first-generation industrial designers. In 1927, after a successful career as an influential stage designer, he opened one of the first industrial design offices in New York City. Geddes is best known for his designs of fantastic streamlined vehicles and for his General Motors Futurama exhibit at the New York World's Fair 1939–1940, an amusement ride visited by millions who viewed a vast miniaturised world of the future dominated by highways, tower cities and automobile consumption. Such designs were guided by his knowledge of the dramatic arts, of intense theatricality and audience manipulation.

This chapter investigates the evolution of and influences on Geddes's design ethos, including Theosophy, Christian Science, advertising theory, psychology and socialism. It illustrates how theatricality was fundamental in his work. His intention was to impress, excite and transform consumers of spectacles, services and products. Geddes's designs were meant to arouse audience's emotions in order to create receptivity to political and commercial messages and facilitate 'spiritual' or 'psychological' transformation, terms he used interchangeably. Though many of these designs were not realised, Geddes's architectural plans and completed projects found influence through their wide dissemination in exhibitions, trade journals, the popular press and his own publications.

In his monograph *Horizons*, 1932, he expressed his long-held hope for the development of an innovative theatrical form characterised by the 'rousing of vast, overwhelming tides of thought and feeling in the masses'.[1] In the mid- to late 1920s Geddes expressed his ideas of emotionally intense and transformative drama in his New York stage design course.[2] In 1929 he wrote, 'every person of vision, without exception, is fascinated by possibilities of this unknown, the unexplored, the state of emotion and ecstasy, which is psychological'.[3] At this time Geddes and other theatrical artists aimed to facilitate in audiences an ecstatic experience of intense rapture. In 1929, he wrote that the dramatist, like the ancient Greeks, should play one dramatic element 'against the other until from their own friction they would burst into flame, [and] drama would attain such power as it has never known'.[4] Geddes was aware of the ancient Greek concept of 'catharsis', the purification of the soul through intense emotional experience.[5] Sheldon Cheney, the prolific theatre journalist and friend of Geddes, was also aware of cathartic theatre. In 1929 he wrote that the 'response' one 'felt' after Greek tragedy was of having been 'purged by experience, taken beyond the world, left with a deeper ecstasy that clarified.'[6] During this period psychoanalysts offered a form of therapeutic catharsis, the release and eradication of damaging emotions linked to traumatic childhood memories thought to be the cause of many psychological problems.[7]

Geddes's knowledge of psychology, advertising theory, Christian Science and Theosophy

Geddes hoped to transform viewers of his designs by breaking down barriers within a variety of spheres: in the theatre between audiences and actors; in the mind between repression and expression; in society between the classes; and in consumer culture between the purchaser and the product. An early source of Geddes's awareness of self-transformation and the blurring of conceptual boundaries was his childhood experience with Christian Science, which taught of a collective unconscious, religious transformation, and the healing power of the mind over the body. Both Geddes's mother and Belle Sneider, his wife of 1916, were adherents of Christian Science. As a child Geddes witnessed his mother's use of prayer to 'heal' his brother.[8] This experience taught Geddes the power of the mind to transform one's self and others, and would guide his knowledge of audience manipulation and consumer engineering.

Geddes's understanding of the persuasive power of design was influenced by his knowledge of advertising, having been an advertising director in the mid-1910s in Detroit and Chicago.[9] In the first decades of the twentieth century, American advertising texts reflected psychological theory.[10] From the 1910s to the 1930s, drama, psychology and transformation were essential aspects of salesmanship. In her study of advertising literature from these decades, Rachel Bowlby writes that the 'sale' was 'a drama, in the full, theatrical sense ...' and its close was equivalent to a moment of 'conversion'.[11] Like Freud's and Joseph Breuer's talking cure, the drama of the sale aimed to create a cathartic change in the subject.[12] In *Consumer Engineering: a New Technique for Prosperity*, 1932, a book on salesmanship that Geddes owned, the authors suggest that consumer engineers should be knowledgeable of the 'deeper and subtler' problems, such as sublimated instincts, dealt with by psychologists.[13] Geddes also owned *The Metropolis of Tomorrow*, 1929, by the architect and architectural renderer Hugh Ferris. In it Ferris stated that 'psychological', especially expressive, honest architecture, had an effect beyond function and 'aesthetics'.[14] Through his books on advertising, psychology and architecture, Geddes encountered ideas, which emphasised the mechanics of thoughts and emotions. He applied such knowledge in his later designs.

By 1918 Geddes was beginning a career as a successful stage designer in New York City.[15] In the 1920s and 1930s New York artists and writers actively explored Spiritualism, Marxism, Freudian theory, Harlem jazz and modernist art.[16] Artists who knew of Freud's theories of the unconscious understood the expression of repressed feelings as an essential aspect of the modernist project.[17] Geddes's designs depended upon his knowledge of emotional, psychological and spiritual transformation, and expressed a belief that design could provide a therapeutic experience. It could alleviate what he and many of his contemporaries viewed as a spiritual malaise within an increasingly mechanised world. The idea that consumption could be stimulated through the release of repressed desires would have had great appeal, especially after the 1929 stock-market crash.

Geddes's knowledge of psychology and spiritual matters was further informed by a long friendship with Claude Bragdon, an architect, set designer, and theosophist whom he met in 1921.[18] In 1922 Bragdon wrote that Geddes's theatre designs, through their combination of light, colour, movement and architecture could release in the viewer 'great primal orgiastic tides of thought and feeling'.[19] Bragdon combined ideas from Theosophy, Spiritualism, psychology, and fourth-dimensional mathematics in order to encourage the spectator's 'ecstatic' experience, a life-altering and intense feeling of mystical absorption and rapturous transcendence.[20]

Geddes owned Bragdon's 1918 book *Architecture and Democracy* in which the theosophist argued that colour, light and movement, especially their combination, had spiritual and healing effects, a concept which accorded with Theosophy.[21] Bragdon thought that the spiritual nature of humankind was repressed and its release would have a therapeutic effect.[22] By 1928 Geddes recommended Bragdon's writing on Theosophy and architecture to his stage-design students.[23] In 1929 Geddes described what he viewed as the primordial 'psychological' effect of colour. He wrote that 'Color [is a] far more emotional power than shape. To an animal or savage it is [a] primal instinct for emotional feeling'.[24] In his 1929 stage-design course Geddes urged his students to 'compose' with colour using rhythm and crescendo.

Bragdon was a leading promoter of fourth-dimensional mathematics and 'higher space' philosophy, and saw a central role for theatrical lighting as an aid to access the dimension 'beyond the tyranny of appearances' where he believed all past and present consciousness was merged.[25] 'With light, as with God … "all things are possible." The drama may unfold itself, not in two, but in all dimensions, unrestricted by any confining boundary.'[26] Bragdon's highest goal was to facilitate access to this realm through the evolution of one's consciousness. In Geddes's 1913 copy of Bragdon's *A Primer of Higher Space (the Fourth Dimension)* he underlined the passage, 'the whole evolutionary process consists in the conquest, dimension by dimension, of successive space-worlds'.[27] In his stage-design lectures of 1927 Geddes wrote, 'the fourth dimension is undefinable [*sic*] to us. This undefinableness [*sic*] is the same quality as in art'.[28]

In 1929 Geddes expressed the view that drama was a necessary aid for travelling beyond ordinary experience, an idea known particularly through expressionist theatre.[29] He believed that 'What the theater needs is drama, not tricks. It needs minds capable of penetrating through the surface of life to its soul and giving out this expression …'[30] It was Bragdon's embrace of the therapeutic use of colour and light, fourth-dimensional theory and ecstatic catharsis that appealed to Geddes as a designer.

Theater #6, 1922: merging the audience and the actors

In 1928 Cheney wrote that the theatre of the last decade had emphasised the unity of theatrical elements in order to achieve the 'highest emotional intensity' for its audience. Cheney wrote that the stage designers who led this trend were Geddes, Lee Simonson, and E. Gordon Craig.[31] Designed to remove any physical barriers between audience and actors and thus encourage an emotional viewing experience, Geddes's plan for Theater #6 has been recognised as an early and influential example of the 'New Stagecraft' in America, a reform trend inspired by European theatre visionaries such as E. Gordon Craig and Adolphe Appia. The new tendency in American theatre emphasised visual design, 'simplified realism', the integration of theatrical elements such as lighting, staging, movement and a more unified theatrical space between the actors and the audience.[32]

Throughout his career Geddes played a role in designing numerous theatres. After 1914, his designs were published in newspapers, architecture and theatre journals, as well as in his own publications. In 1920 Geddes's highly influential design for the production of Dante's *Divine Comedy* helped to secure his international reputation as a theatrical visionary.[33] The unrealised *Divine Comedy* was to use two 70-foot towers, platforms, a pit stage, masses of moving actors, and innovative lighting often used in place of scenery.[34] Geddes first exhibited his plans for Theater #6 in 1914, refining the design by 1922. In plan, the stage appears as a quarter circle placed in the corner of a square. From the curved edge of the stage a series of aisles radiate at diagonals. The interior ceiling above the stage was a large dome and could be lit to intensify the mood. The plan synthesised many of Geddes's key theatrical ideas, including the rejection of the traditional proscenium arch in order to integrate audience and actors, the projection of lights from behind the audience for non-invasive, mood-enhancing effects and hydraulic stages for seamless scenery changes.[35]

In his 1922 review of Theatre #6, Bragdon claimed that Geddes's application of light illustrated the medium's ability to act as an 'emotional language, like music, with power to induce and maintain moods of the soul'.[36] Bragdon wrote that the nearest things to such a theatre were 'the revival meeting, the prize fight, or the ball game' – religious and commercial spheres, which Bragdon believed were only partially able to provide an intense response.[37] In his review Bragdon showed an awareness of psychoanalytic theory and explained that Geddes's theatre architecture would help to direct 'repressed' feelings into outlets of creativity and inspiration. 'These great forces [repressed feelings] … are destined to re-enter life either in the shape of mob-violence – as a result of repression – or through inspiration to creative effort, if they find a prepared and natural channel such as theatre.'[38] In accord with Geddes and the New Stagecraft, Bragdon believed that the removal of physical barriers between the stage and auditorium would create a sense of communion between the spectators and the actors. Combining social unity with the impact of the drama 'would promote a feeling … [in which] … spectators become responsive, impressionable, enthusiastic, sensitive to every emotional overtone'.[39] Bragdon suggested that this state of responsiveness and impressionability would encourage a psychological and spiritual transformation.

Geddes's stage-design lectures, 1924–1929

In his New York stage-design lectures Geddes claimed that effective design depended upon the viewer's emotional and psychological metamorphosis. He defined 'pure drama' as a 'sequence of movement acting upon [the] mind & capable of stirring it emotionally'.[40] He felt that rhythmic lighting had a 'powerful', 'psychological' and 'hypnotic' effect.[41] Not surprisingly, when discussing the effects of colour Geddes credited Bragdon.[42] Both of these men were captivated by the synaesthetic performances in the early 1920s of a keyboard that projected brilliant patterns of dancing light, Thomas Wilfred's 'color organ', or 'Clavilux', which was later performed at the Exposition des Arts Décoratifs in Paris in 1925.[43]

The idea of combining various media into an expressive and unified art form appealed to Geddes and Bragdon who longed for an art of great intensity, unburdened by intellectual and aesthetic boundaries. They may have seen the Clavilux as an attempt to fulfil E. Gordon Craig's 'prophesy' of a 'new religion' of light.[44] In 1918 Bragdon wrote, 'Indeed, with the aid of light, the theater may be the nursery of a new art-form altogether, a synthesis of sound, form, color, and mobility'.[45] Describing the potential of the Clavilux in 1922, Bragdon revealed his distaste for the use of colour and light as a commercial medium. He wrote of 'that Art of the future of which Wilfred's Clavilux gave us the first faint actual intimation, showing what colored light might become when disassociated from all those ideas of corsets, chewing-gum, automobile tires, etcetera'.[46]

It was on this crucial point that Geddes diverged from Bragdon. In 1920 Geddes was internationally celebrated as a theatrical visionary for his designs of Dante's *Divine Comedy*; however, by the end of the decade he increasingly engaged in commercial design, including his designs of steel furniture for the Simmons Company, weighing scales for the Toledo Scale Company, and automobiles for the Graham-Paige Company. While Bragdon advocated the use of intensity, light, colour and movement for primarily spiritual and therapeutic ends, Geddes applied the same techniques to achieve concrete economic results. The spaces where he directed his commercial dramas were the Franklin Simon window displays of 1927–1929, the J. Walter Thompson advertising agency assembly hall of 1929 and the Aerial Restaurant of 1929 for the Chicago World's Fair of 1933/34. Through these projects, Geddes was not concerned with spiritual or artistic rapture for its own sake, but aimed to bring about commercial conversion. Dramatic design could lead as much to religious ecstasy as to the closing of the sale.

Franklin Simon window displays, 1927–1929 and the J. Walter Thompson Assembly Hall, 1929

With his designs of window displays, 1927–1929, for the Franklin Simon department store, Geddes continued his move from theatre to industrial design, applying his knowledge of drama to the sphere of consumer goods. The historian William Leach has recognised window display as fundamental to American consumer society in the early twentieth century, viewing it as an essential site of fantasy, theatre, technological play and consumption.[47] The combination of these elements was important to Geddes's theatrical design and would become essential in his commercial projects. In 1932 Geddes wrote that 'the store window is a stage on which the merchandise is presented as the actors'.[48] The window must 'arrest the glance; focus attention upon the merchandise; persuade the onlooker to desire it'.[49] Like a theatre set, Geddes's Franklin Simon window displays spotlighted the products. They employed a background that graduated from beige to dark grey, thus creating a neutral setting for the central character – the product. The display platform was made of modular triangular components, which could be constructed in twelve shades of yellow, blue or red.

2.1 Franklin Simon window display, 1929, designed by Norman Bel Geddes.

2.2 J. Walter Thompson Advertising Agency assembly hall, 1929, designed by Norman Bel Geddes.

According to Geddes, the window attracted huge crowds and such dramatic window display had a 'psychological' effect essential in selling products.[50]

After his work in window displays, Geddes continued his foray into the design of commercial spaces. In 1929 Stanley Resor, the president of J. Walter Thompson, the era's leading advertising agency, commissioned Geddes to design the conference room of their New York office (see Figure 2.2). The design required Geddes to produce an 'unusual' space that 'immediately' created 'a favourable impression' upon clients and board members.[51] The result was a large hall – eighty by thirty feet in area and twenty-five feet high – that used subtle lighting, a dramatic space and elegant materials to create an impressive effect. The walls were oyster grey and employed concealed ceiling lights operated by dimmers. From floor to ceiling ran tall windows, strips of brass, turquoise curtains and black Vitrolite, an opaque structural glass.[52] The theatrical effect of the room was noted by one reviewer in *Theatre Arts Monthly*, who wrote of its 'power and drama'.[53] Geddes recognised the importance of design in managing a company's image and moulding a client's mood, noting that an effective office 'should put the visitor in a receptive, cooperative frame of mind'.[54]

From stage design to architecture: plans for the Chicago World's Fair

During the late 1920s Geddes had considered his role in theatre in architectural terms.[55] In 1928 Cheney described the 'architectural' qualities of his stage sets.[56] In his 1932 book, the stage designer Lee Simonson described Geddes's theatre sets as 'purely architectural compositions'.[57] After 1916 Geddes attempted an ultimately unsuccessful collaboration with Frank Lloyd Wright on Aline Barnsdall's Los Angeles Little Theatre.[58] In 1924 he began a long friendship with the German architect of expressionist buildings Eric Mendelsohn, who gave him a copy of his book *Structures and Sketches* and a drawing of his Einstein Tower.[59] In his introduction to Mendelsohn's work in the catalogue for the 1929 Contempora Exposition of Art and Industry, Geddes wrote that enduring architecture depended upon drama and emotion, that the ideal architect 'with the dramatist's instinct ... adds the emotional quality that attracts and inspires humanity for all time'.[60] This view would guide Geddes's approach to architecture.

Geddes's reputation as a designer of novel buildings is based to a large degree on a group of eight designs of theatres and restaurants, including a rotating tower restaurant, developed for the Chicago World's Fair of 1933. The group of buildings grew out of an earlier plan for the fair, an attempt to develop a non-commercial, avant-garde theatre movement for a mass audience. In July 1929 Geddes was invited to develop an innovative theatrical program for the Chicago World's Fair.[61] His plan was to showcase the talent of the world's best modern theatrical artists within a group of theatres of his own design. Geddes sent letters to leading directors, stage designers, producers, architects, artists and writers, asking them to dream up their own ideal non-commercial theatre.[62] Included among those contacted were Cheney, Jean Cocteau, Jacques Copeau, E. Gordon Craig, Robert Edmund Jones, Eugene O'Neil, Pablo Picasso, Luigi Pirandello, Max Reinhardt, Oskar Schlemmer, Constantin Stanislavsky and Frank Lloyd Wright.[63] Though Geddes hoped his plan might bring intense theatre and dramatic architecture to an even larger audience, after the 1929 stock-market crash the fair developed a more commercial emphasis and his plans were left unfulfilled.

In February 1930 Geddes was invited as an advisor to the fair's Architectural Commission.[64] He was asked to design the exterior illumination of the buildings and grounds and to provide 'concrete examples' of a variety of designs for restaurant and theatre architecture.[65] Though Geddes was hired as 'Consultant for Illuminations', he was aware that his new job was a theatrical one, requiring him to 'dramatize the grounds'.[66] This was an opportunity for the designer to achieve his and Bragdon's hopes for light as a new and unfulfilled aesthetic expression. One of Geddes's designs showed a group of dramatically lit 'great piers' upon which were the words, 'In the beginning there was light'.[67] Another sketch illustrated a hydrogen-filled, translucent dome containing a 'fountain of light' that distorted and projected the 'shadows' of the viewing crowds.[68] Geddes's World's Fair illumination plans illustrated his continuing interest in dissolving the barrier between viewer and performer by integrating the audience with a dramatic spectacle.

2.3 Aerial restaurant, 1929, designed by Norman Bel Geddes for the Chicago World's Fair of 1933–1934.

The Aerial Restaurant was one of Geddes's eight designs for the fair of novel restaurants and theatres, which ranged from the intimate to the monumental (see Figure 2.3). The plan of the Aerial Restaurant illustrated his flair for infusing architecture with drama. The design of the rotating tower restaurant was for a 278-foot-tall structure with a steel shaft supporting a three-level, cantilevered platform. The revolving three levels were for dining and dancing for up to 1,200 people. Each of the levels was made of aluminium and glass. The restaurants had floor-to-ceiling glass windows surrounded by open-air terraces. The interior floors and exterior terraces were stepped to accommodate viewing of the Chicago skyline.

The design of the building was technological, dynamic, and commercial – a spectacular synthesis of Geddes's knowledge of drama, advertising, and modernist architecture. Like the engineering feats of previous fairs, such as the Eiffel Tower of the Paris Exposition Universelle of 1889, the Aerial Restaurant is an example of the 'techno-logical sublime', technology that induces an intense emotional response, a primarily religious feeling, in its audience.[69] As its name indicated, the Aerial Restaurant combined both sublime and carnal experiences – a dizzying panorama of the fairgrounds and the city of Chicago below, accompanied by food and dancing. One contemporary commentator considered the Aerial Restaurant 'a little mad'.[70] However, it was the influence of the theatre which was seen as the most significant aspect of the design: 'at least we have here experiments untrammelled by reverence for that tradition of the theater which has been too powerful so far for even our most courageous architects'.[71] Geddes has given two reasons why his plans for the Chicago fair were never realised – the stock-market crash and pressure from registered architects.[72]

The Kharkov Theater, Ukraine design proposal, 1931

Geddes's designs and rhetoric of the early 1930s reflected the fascination with socialist ideology among America's liberal artists and intellectuals.[73] Many of the ideas of Theater #6 were echoed in Geddes's design proposal of 1931 for the Kharkov Theater, including the removal of the proscenium arch, the emphasis on lighting effects and, most importantly, the merging of audience and actors, or in this

2.4 Ukranian State Theatre, Kharkov, 1931, designed by Norman Bel Geddes.

case, the proletariat and socialist ideology (see Figure 2.4). The design was intended to excite, transform, and make audiences responsive to socialist thought. It also expressed the designer's belief in the effectiveness of drama as a means of conveying a concept. In *Horizons* Geddes wrote, 'There is no more emphatic way of bringing an idea to the attention of a mass audience and doing it with great force and conviction than in the theater.'[74]

Geddes was excited by the political, economic, and aesthetic ideas emanating from Soviet Russia. He owned many books on socialist theatre, the Russian Revolution and Lenin spanning 1924–1934. In *Horizons* he expressed his belief that the economic answers to America's seemingly out-of-control business culture might be found in post-revolutionary Russian planning.[75] Significantly, the Kharkov Theatre design brief was in accord with Geddes's own design goals – dramatising an idea in order to provoke an emotional and intellectual response, and to unite the performers and the audience. The prospectus for the theatre competition opened with the words, 'Workers of the World, UNITE!', and emphasised the need for a theatre design which would, 'according to its style and technique, reflect in its architectural forms … proletarian culture … the industrialization of the country, [and] socialist reconstruction of all Public Economy and in all domains of culture'.[76] It called for external balconies for orators, arrangements for lighting effects and the mixing of actors and audience '[in] correspondence with ideological demands'.[77] Geddes's theatre plan met the brief, amplified the design concepts developed for Theater #6, and reflected the enormous scale of his theatre designs for the Chicago World's Fair. His Kharkov Theater design combined three theatres into one structure, including a monumental 'Mass Theater' with a seating capacity of 60,000 and the potential for up to 5,000 actors.[78] The design of the indoor theatre included a ramp that would enable actors to merge with the audience.[79] All three stages allowed for illumination effects and sound amplification.[80] Geddes published his designs in *Horizons*, but did not win the competition. According to Geddes, he received second prize in the Kharkov Theater competition, and the 'Theatre, as built, in 1936, followed my design almost in its entirety, though a Russian is credited as having won it'.[81]

Though Geddes had a keen interest in Russian culture and its planned economy, the possibility of adapting the techniques of Soviet mass spectacle to his own commercial work particularly attracted his interest. Through his participation in the design of the Kharkov Theater Geddes practised a form of cultural and technological exchange. By the 1920s Russia had imported American management theories and production technologies, in the form of Taylorism and Fordism, to improve its industrial and economic capacity.[82] Conversely, Geddes imported Russian 'technologies' of mass spectacle which could further American capitalist goals. In his commercial designs for mass audiences, such as the Futurama, Geddes would use architecture as an ideological medium. His Futurama exhibition expressed capitalist ideology, encouraging automobile ownership, technological progress and the moulding of passive spectators into active consumers.

Conclusion

In 1924 Gilbert Seldes published *The Seven Lively Arts*, a 'radical aesthetic manifesto' that proclaimed the importance of popular American culture, including musical theatre, jazz, slapstick, the circus and comic strips.[83] For Seldes the lively arts were popular, commercial, and entertaining, but, first and foremost, they were 'intense'.[84] In his book Seldes included Geddes's stage designs as a significant contribution to the lively arts.[85] Geddes knew of Seldes's ideas and owned his book, and by 1930 was his theatrical collaborator.[86] Throughout *Horizons* Geddes associated his designs with mass appeal, intensity and theatricality. He recognised that design required theatricality in order to compete with existing forms of popular culture. He wrote, 'unquestionably, a new liveliness is coming into architecture and we may yet hear of it as one of the Seven Lively Arts. It can certainly be made as vivacious as the tabloids, the talkies, or vaudeville'.[87]

Geddes's designs of window displays and architecture grew out of his knowledge of theatre, with its emphasis on intense drama and audience transformation. Geddes believed that theatre had a direct impact on audiences and that it provided an important form of mass entertainment and education. His theatrical aesthetic was gathered from a variety of sources, including Christian Science, advertising theory, psychology, socialism and Theosophy, as well as the ideas of Claude Bragdon and Gilbert Seldes. Applicable to both non-commercial projects and the realities of trade, Geddes's use of theatricality in design encouraged the transformation of mere viewers into active consumers of ideology, spectacle and commercial goods.

Notes

1 N. Geddes, *Horizons* (Boston: Little, Brown, 1932), p. 156.

2 The stage design course was given to a small and select group of students, including Henry Dreyfuss, 1922–23. The lectures are dated 1924–1929. Stage Design Course and Book, 1929, file 79, Norman Bel Geddes Archive, Harry Ransom Humanities Research Center, University of Texas, Austin (NBG).

3 Stage Design Course and Book (1929), file 79, p. 2, NBG.

4 'The Objective 4', Stage Design Course and Book (1929), file 79, NBG.

5 G. Wilson, *The Psychology of the Performing Arts* (New York: St. Martin's Press, 1985), p. 3.

6 S. Cheney, *The Theatre: Three Thousand Years of Drama, Acting and Stagecraft* (New York: Longmans, Green, 1952 [1929]), p. 537. In 1916 Cheney founded *Theatre Arts Magazine*, the main disseminator of new theatre ideas until 1948.

7   Wilson, *Psychology*, pp. 33–5.

8   M.B. Eddy was the founder of Christian Science, and Geddes owned her book, *Science and Health: with a Key to the Scriptures* (Boston: A.V. Stewart, 1914), signed presentation copy of Christmas 1913 to Geddes from his mother, Geddes monogram with date 1914, 'Norman M. Geddes' written in hand underneath. W. Kelley (ed.), *Miracle in the Evening: An Autobiography of Norman Bel Geddes* (Garden City, NY: Doubleday, 1960), pp. 28–9.

9   Kelley, *Miracle in the Evening*, pp. 140–9.

10 See J. Lears, *Fables of Abundance: A Cultural History of Advertising in America* (New York: Basic Books, 1994).

11 R. Bowlby, *Shopping with Freud* (London: Routledge, 1993), p. 109.

12 J. Breuer and S. Freud, *Studies in Hysteria*, intro. A.A. Brill (Boston: Beacon, 1960 [1895]).

13 E. Arens and R. Sheldon, *Consumer Engineering: a New Technique for Prosperity* (New York: Harper and Brothers, 1932), pp. 97–100, 19, miscellaneous markings by Geddes, NBG.

14 H. Ferris, *The Metropolis of Tomorrow* (New York: I. Washburn, 1929), pp. 60, 61, stamped 'this book belongs in the library of Norman Bel Geddes', NBG.

15 G.T. Hellman, 'Profiles: Design for a Living-II', *New Yorker* (15 February 1941), p. 24.

16 T. Bender, *New York Intellect: a History of Intellectual Life in New York City, from 1750 to the Beginnings of Our Own Time* (New York: Alfred A. Knopf, 1987), p. 228. See also H.F. May, *The Discontent of the Intellectuals: A Problem of the Twenties* (Chicago: Rand McNally, 1963); C. Lasch, *The New Radicalism in America: [1889–1963] The Intellectual as a Social Type* (New York: Alfred A. Knopf, 1966).

17 A. Douglas, *Terrible Honesty: Mongrel Manhattan in the 1920s* (London: Papermac, 1997).

18 Letter from C. Bragdon to Geddes, 29 April 1921, file 957, NBG.

19 Summary of article by C. Bragdon, *Architectural Record*, 52: (3 September 1922), serial no. 288, pp. 171–82, Theater #6 Clippings, file 15, NBG.

20 C. Bragdon, *The Frozen Fountain: Being Essays on Architecture and the Art of Design in Space* (New York: Knopf, 1932), pp. 6, 8; L.D. Henderson, *The Fourth Dimension and Non-Euclidean Geometry in Modern Art* (Princeton, NJ: Princeton University Press, 1983); Bragdon, *The Frozen Fountain*, p. 8.

21 C. Bragdon, *Architecture and Democracy* (New York: Alfred A. Knopf, 1918), p. 68; Cheney, *The New World Architecture* (London: Longmans,

Green and Co., 1930). Cheney thought highly of Bragdon's architectural and theatrical work. Cheney, *Stage Decoration* (London: Chapman & Hall, 1928), pp. 215–18. Geddes owned a copy of Cheney's *New World Architecture*, 1930, which has tipped-in notes from Cheney dated May and June 1931, NBG.

22 Bragdon, *The Frozen Fountain*, pp. 50, 57, 66, 6.

23 Stage Design Course, 79, Cabinet (SC–6), Folder y.3, Frances Waite Resor's class notes, 1927–8, NBG.

24 Advanced Course – Dramatization of Color – (Visible and Audible) – Lesson VII, Stage Design Course and Book, 1929, file 79, NBG.

25 C. Bragdon, *Four-Dimensional Vistas* (New York: Alfred A. Knopf, 1916), p. 9.

26 C. Bragdon, *Merely Players* (New York: Alfred A. Knopf, 1929), p. 39.

27 C. Bragdon, *A Primer of Higher Space (the Fourth Dimension)* (Rochester: The Manas Press, 1913), miscellaneous notes throughout, p. 21, NBG.

28 'Draft of Stage Design Book', ca. 1927, Stage Design Course and Book, file 79, NBG.

29 The theatrical presentation of an alternate psychological reality had been central to German Expressionist theatre of the 1910s and 1920s. S. Behr, D. Fanning and J. Douglas, *Expressionism Reassessed* (Manchester: Manchester University Press, 1993), p. 2.

30 Stage Design Course and Book, ca. 1929, file 79, NBG.

31 Cheney, *Stage Decoration*, p. 10.

32 R. Leacroft and H. Lea, *Theatre and Playhouse: an Illustrated Survey of Theatre Building from Ancient Greece to the Present Day* (London: Methuen, 1984); O.G. Brockett, *History of Theatre* (Boston: Allyn and Bacon, 1982 [1968]), pp. 625–7.

33 Brockett, *History of Theatre*, p. 627; Cheney, *The Theatre: Three Thousand Years*, p. 534.

34 M. Banham, *The Cambridge Guide to Theater* (Cambridge: Cambridge University Press, 1995), p. 83; Cheney, *The Theatre: Three Thousand Years*, p. 534.

35 Geddes's designs for theatres were reproduced and celebrated in many contemporary and recent theatre histories, including W.R. Fuerst and S.J. Hume, *Twentieth-Century Stage Decoration*, Vol. 1 (New York: Benjamin Blom, 1967 [1929]); Cheney, *The Theatre: Three Thousand Years*; Brockett, *History of Theatre*.

36 Bragdon, *Architectural Record*, p. 182.

37 Ibid.

38 Ibid.

39 Ibid.

40 'Advanced Course – Drama, Its Form and Quality – Lesson III (Play & the Stage)', Stage Design Course and Book, ca. 1929, file 79, NBG.

41 Stage Design Course and Book, ca. 1927, file 79, pp. 33–10, NBG.

42 Under 'color' Geddes referred to Bragdon's translation of Ouspensky's, *Tertium Organum*, NBG.

43 On Wilfred see W. Moritz, 'Abstract Film and Colour Music', in M. Tuchman et al., *The Spiritual in Art: Abstract Painting, 1890–1985* (New York: Abbeville, 1986), pp. 298, 299.

44 Simonson quoted from L. Simonson, *The Stage is Set* (New York: Harcourt, Brace, 1932), pp. 62, 327.

45 C. Bragdon, *Merely Players* (New York: Alfred A. Knopf, 1929), p. 39, a collection of Bragdon's writing spanning 1905–29.

46 Bragdon, *Architectural Record* 52(3), September 1922, serial no. 288, p. 180.

47 W. Leach, 'Strategists of Display and the Production of Desire', in S.J. Bronner (ed.), *Consuming Visions: Accumulation and Display of Goods in America, 1880–1920* (New York: W.W. Norton, 1989), pp. 100–10.

48 Geddes, *Horizons*, p. 259.

49 Ibid.

50 Ibid., p. 243.

51 Transcripts of articles on J. Walter Thompson assembly room, stamped 26 August 1954; transcript of R. Peters article in *N.Y. Evening Post*, in Autobiography, AE75, Chapter 71, both NBG.

52 Ibid.

53 Article transcript from *Theatre Arts Monthly*, Autobiography, AE75, Chapter 71, NBG.

54 J.W. Thompson Office, 11 May 1955, Autobiography, AE75, Chapter 71, file 71, NBG.

55 'Draft of Stage Design Book', Stage Design Course and Book, 1927, file 79, NBG.

56 Cheney, *Stage Decoration*, pp. 119, 98

57 L. Simonson, *The Stage is Set*, pp. 62, 344.

58 J. Meikle, *Twentieth Century Limited* (Philadelphia, PA: Temple University Press, 1979), p. 48.

59 Ibid., p. 49; E. Mendelsohn, *Structures and Sketches* (Berlin: Ernst Wasmuth,

no date). The book and sketch pasted in the front cover are dated 25 November 1924 by Mendelsohn.

60 Meikle, *Twentieth Century Limited*, p. 49.

61 Letter to Geddes from A.D. Albert, 11 July 1929, Chicago World's Fair Advisory Commission correspondence, NBG.

62 Letter from Geddes to A.D. Albert, 2 July 1929, Chicago World's Fair Advisory Commission correspondence; letter from Geddes to 'outstanding individuals ...' 23 October 1929; letters in response to Geddes, August 1929–March 1930, NBG.

63 The list of those who were sent letters also included Harley Granville Barker, Paul Green, Sidney Howard, Leopold Jessner, Louis Jouvet, Georg Kaiser, Emil Pirchan, Georges Pitoëff, and Alexander Tairov. Ibid., NBG.

64 Letter to Geddes from H.W. Corbett, 10 February 1930, Chicago World's Fair Illuminating Plans, file 182, NBG; *Horizons*, p. 161.

65 Geddes, *Horizons*, p. 161; letter to Geddes from Corbett, 10 February 1930, file 182, NBG.

66 M.K. Wisehart, 'Are YOU Afraid of the Unexpected', *American Magazine* (July 1931), pp. 71–3, 85. Publicity, file 937, NBG.

67 Illumination Plan, Preliminary Sketches, file 182, NBG.

68 Ibid.

69 D. Nye, *American Technological Sublime* (Cambridge, MA: MIT Press, 1994).

70 Summary transcript of untitled and undated newspaper article, ca. 1930–3, Publicity Clippings, file 147, NBG.

71 Ibid.

72 Geddes, *Horizons*, p. 162.

73 May, *Discontent of the Intellectuals*; Lasch, *New Radicalism in America*.

74 Geddes, *Horizons*, p. 156.

75 Ibid., p. 289.

76 This quote has been underlined by Geddes. 'Prospectus for the International Competition in Composing a Project for the State Ukrainian Theater Mass Musical Stage with 4,000 Seat Capacity', ca. June 1931, p. 117, file 203, NBG.

77 Ibid., pp. 119, 128.

78 Letter to Geddes from Kostrov and M. Liubtchenko, 31 June 1931, file 203, NBG.

79 Geddes, *Horizons*, p. 140.

80 'A Project for the State Theater of the Ukraine', file 203, NBG.

81 Letter to W.K. Harrison, New York, New York, from Geddes (27 April 1957), NBG.

82 Translations of F.W. Taylor's writing on scientific management spread throughout Europe prior to World War I. Fordism was even more popular, especially in Russia in the 1920s.

83 M. Kammen, *American Culture, American Tastes: Social Change and the Twentieth Century* (New York: Alfred A. Knopf, 1999) p. 220; G. Seldes, *The Seven Lively Arts* (New York: Harper & Brothers, 1924).

84 M. Kammen, *The Lively Arts: Gilbert Seldes and the Transformation of Cultural Criticism in the United States* (Oxford: Oxford University Press, 1996), pp. 25, 9; Seldes, *The Seven Lively Arts*, p. 318.

85 Ibid., p. 313.

86 Geddes's copy includes tipped-in notes from Seldes to Geddes dated April and May 1930, NBG. In April of 1930 Geddes directed and designed Seldes's version of *Lysistrata*, which opened in Philadelphia. F.J. Hunter, *Catalog of the Norman Bel Geddes Theater Collection, Humanities Research Center University of Texas at Austin* (Boston: G.K. Hall & Co., 1973), p. 13.

87 Geddes, *Horizons*, p. 186.

3 ✧ The construction of a modern pleasure palace: Dreamland Cinema, Margate, 1935

Josephine Kane

DREAMLAND, Margate, was a successful and influential amusement complex, which opened in 1919 on the site of a Victorian entertainment venue known as the Hall-by-the-Sea. Within a decade, the new owner John Henry Iles (1872–1951) had transformed Dreamland into the most significant entertainment site in the south of England. It boasted a 20-acre amusement park with roller coasters and other mechanised rides, a speedway track, zoo, cinema, ballroom, landscaped gardens and promenades, and several restaurants, cafés and licensed bars.[1]

The success of Dreamland rested on its ability to cater to the tastes of the predominantly working-class Londoners who visited Margate in huge numbers. As a provider of mass entertainment operating within a period of major social change, Dreamland is a rich and untapped area of study, firmly rooted in the history of popular leisure, mechanised amusements and the British seaside. Despite the peripheral location of Margate, both geographically and intellectually, the themes raised in this chapter, such as notions of modernity and the experience of cinema going, are central to the social and cultural history of Britain during the 1930s.

In the field of design history, the study of an amusement park might appear problematic. Rather than a system of objects, Dreamland is viewed as a designed environment, which may be understood as a composite of multiple (often chaotic) elements, consumed through the senses of the visitor as much as by physical use. For the purposes of this chapter, I will focus on one important aspect of Dreamland, the cinema that opened in March 1935.[2] The new 2,200-seater supercinema with its state-of-the-art facilities and pioneering architectural form marked a pivotal moment in the history of Dreamland and its transformation from provincial seaside amusement park to modern pleasure complex of national repute.[3]

The cinema, together with the investment of over half a million pounds in the park, amounted to the reinvention of Dreamland. The success and publicity surrounding the new building propelled its architects to the forefront of English Modernism, while securing John Henry Iles's place among the leading entrepreneurs of contemporary British entertainment. This chapter explores the significance of the cinema, both architecturally and in relation to the park and rides which lay behind it. It also considers the expectations and experiences of visitors, aiming to set Dreamland within the wider context of British leisure and society during the inter-war period.

Context: Dreamland and leisure for the masses

The 1920s and 1930s were a time of economic contrast. Many Britons faced an era of depression and unemployment, while others enjoyed their first taste of affluence. Those regions dependent on the old staple industries, such as coal, cotton and shipbuilding, were hit hard by international competition and the disruption of the First World War. In contrast, the 'new' industries, such as car manufacture, electrical appliances and food processing, which were based around London and the Midlands, experienced impressive expansion.[4] On average, real wages increased, working hours shortened and family size fell, meaning that, overall, quality of life improved.[5] Higher disposable incomes and increased free time meant that personal consumption in many areas grew and was reflected in, among other things, an increase in leisure activities and commercial entertainment.[6]

A major repercussion of this trend was the establishment of the annual holiday as a standard component of British working life. Leisure was viewed not merely as compensation for labour, but as a potential means of recovering the eroded values of family and community, and of instilling political ideals.[7] Popular seaside resorts which featured American-style mechanised amusements, such as

Blackpool and Margate, aroused considerable anxiety about the state of working-class leisure. For the Mass Observers who studied Blackpool in 1937, such resorts were a 'symbol of the modernised primitivism of the passive working classes'.[8] Similarly, J.B. Priestley distinguished between those who preferred invigorating countryside recreations to mass entertainment, and the 'less intelligent and enterprising', those 'patrons of the New Blackpool, which knows what to do with the passive and listless'.[9]

During the inter-war period, Margate benefited not only from the general increase of holiday making and leisure expenditure among the working classes, but also from the boom in light industry which brought increased affluence to London and the surrounding districts. At Easter 1933 approximately 10,000 more visitors came to Margate than in the previous year.[10] This was partly because many of the new expanding industries of the south-east organised their work outings at Margate, which became famous for its mass catering during the 1930s. While the decade saw a general decline in the quantity of longer-stay holidaymakers to the resort, the numbers of day-trippers sharply increased, and the town's prosperity was reflected in its expansion.[11]

Dreamland also prospered during the 1920s and early 1930s, augmenting its catering facilities and becoming famous for its Beanfeasts, the factory outings which remained popular until the late 1940s. Growing profits were reinvested, increasing the number of attractions, reorganising existing amusements and replacing flimsy wooden structures with brick and concrete.[12] Several new major rides were acquired, though the Scenic Railway roller coaster, built in 1920, remained the star attraction. The Palais-de-Danse ballroom was converted into a 900-seat cinema with its own orchestra in 1923, doubling up as a variety theatre, while the old roller-skating rink was transformed into a large ballroom with Tudor-style decoration.[13]

By the mid-1930s, 200,000 people a day visited Dreamland during the high season.[14] The programme of ongoing improvements was fundamental to the success of Dreamland during its first fifteen years. As a souvenir brochure acknowledged, 'Progress brooks no relaxation of effort. The tastes and appeals of entertainment are constantly changing. The public's demands become more and more exacting'.[15] The continuous acquisition of new rides at Dreamland fulfilled this demand, while updating the park structures and layout reinforced the impression of freshness and modernity.

The entrance front was a crucial element in attracting holiday-makers into Dreamland and, in 1923, the original Victorian façade was developed into an elegant entrance, echoing the traditional style of seaside winter gardens. However, advertising hoardings were gradually added, resulting in a chaotic and aesthetically unbalanced front, and by the later 1920s this entrance fell far short of the modern and exciting image Iles wanted to project to potential customers.

In fact, by 1930, the seafront facilities as a whole were becoming increasingly dilapidated. A major fire in 1932 provided the impetus for further reconstruction. Iles envisaged a building that would provide both an appropriate frontispiece for the updated amusement park and a striking visual stop for the crowds on the seafront. The solution was to build a new complex, incorporating a state-of-the-art supercinema, with stylish cafés, bars and shops, as well as the existing ballroom, in a structure that would attract visitors into the park behind, and become synonymous with an all-new Dreamland experience.

Palaces of dreams: inter-war cinema architecture

There had been cinema shows on the Dreamland site since the beginning of the century, yet popular demand reached new heights in the 1930s. Cinema going was *the* defining cultural activity of the inter-war years in Britain. In 1926, an estimated 3,000 cinemas were in operation, rising to 4,967 by 1938.[16] Annual admissions rose from 903 million in 1934 (the first year for which reliable statistics exist), to a staggering 990 million in 1939.[17] The *New Survey of London Life and Labour* concluded in 1935 that it had become 'par excellence the people's entertainment'.[18] For many, the local cinema assumed a status comparable with that of traditional centres of community life, such as the church and the pub.[19]

Going to the pictures encapsulated a total experience, of which watching a film was only part. The facilities offered by cinemas, partic-ularly the ubiquitous café, were as popular as the films themselves.[20] It is, therefore, not surprising that the buildings themselves took on a heightened significance. During the 1930s, the plain rectangular buildings which had been hurriedly erected during the first cinema boom of the previous decade were gradually replaced by larger, lavishly decorated structures, designed in an array of styles from Jacobean manor houses to Spanish haciendas.[21]

Three cinema-design movements dominated the decade. 1929 saw the arrival in South London of the first 'atmospheric', which simulated the experience of being outdoors in exotic settings, such as an Italian auditorium, or a Moorish walled city. The atmospherics' interiors were characterised by two-dimensional 'buildings', fountains, antique statuary and trailing vines.[22] The second influential style of the era, the spectacular medieval interiors of the Granada cinemas, featured Romanesque arches, ornate balustrades, gothic cloisters and heroic murals.[23]

A stark polarity thus existed between the aesthetics of the traditional pub or club, and the fantastical, romanticised luxury of the new centres of community life. Arising amid the drab surroundings of working-class areas of London (and later other large cities), they proved enormously popular. The Granadas and atmospherics presented America as the image of the modern.[24] This is perhaps significant not only because it echoes trends in other areas of popular entertainment, such as fairgrounds and amusement parks, but also because, in the unstable political and economic climate of the inter-war years, many people feared that Europe was on the brink of radical upheaval. American-style fantasy grandeur, in the form of a medieval castle or an Aztec city, offered not just an escape from the drabness of everyday life, but also a reassuringly nostalgic aesthetic, which underpinned the status quo.

A third and very different architectural style, however, has become synonymous with inter-war cinema design. The Odeon house style was developed by the architects Harry Weedon and Cecil Clavering, and combined the Modernist elements of streamlined curves, clean lines and fin towers, with art deco motifs and night time floodlighting. While sharing similar levels of interior luxury, the Odeons were far less flamboyant in style and construction-cost than the atmospherics and Granadas, and were built in predominantly middle-class suburbs.[25]

It can be argued that the Odeon architects, while still providing escapism, set their cinemas aesthetically apart from the working-class associations of the atmospherics and Granadas, turning from America toward Europe for inspiration (a shift which was first signalled by the new cinema at Dreamland). The Odeon buildings thus embodied a specific set of values, including that of European Modernism, and employed them to evoke associations of middle-class respectability, rationality and improvement. The taste in films of the patrons of these cinemas suggests that such associations would have had considerable appeal. According to a survey of 1937, British and European films were particularly popular with middle-class audiences, as opposed to the fast action or sentimentality seen to characterise American films.[26]

Much has been written on the discourses latent in both American and British films of this era, yet this aspect of the cinema buildings themselves has been largely neglected. In his analysis of the architecture of Blackpool Pleasure Beach in the late nineteenth century, Tony Bennett suggests that the entertainments were imbued with a variety of discourses (such as constructions of regionalism, modernity and imperialism) and were employed to maintain social and cultural hierarchies.[27] It can be argued that the supercinema circuit owners who commissioned the new buildings in the 1920s and 1930s had an important stake in maintaining the political and economic status quo. In this light, the new breeds of cinemas may be seen to represent a 'set of lived ideological relations which the visitor inescapably entered into and breathed in'.[28] It is crucial, therefore, that the often bizarre architecture of inter-war cinemas is not dismissed merely as irrelevant frivolity. Sites of popular leisure and entertainment, such as amusement parks and cinemas, were significant agents of social, cultural and even political life in Britain, exciting widespread academic interest.[29]

Dreamland Cinema: constructing a modern pleasure palace

As well as being part of the grand reinvention of Dreamland, the decision to build a cinema complex must be seen as part of the cinema-building fever that swept Britain during the later 1920s and 1930s. The Dreamland Cinema was just one of 302 built in Britain between 1932 and 1934, including two supercinemas in Margate alone.[30] It was, therefore, crucial to design a structure that would stand out from the multitude. In terms of publicity, profit and value for money, Dreamland had to make a splash in the cinema-building world.

3.1 Dreamland Cinema front, 1934. The dramatic verticality of Dreamland's fin was balanced by the combined horizontal elements of a cantilevered canopy above the street entrances, and the wide expanse of the windows above, which ran in a curvilinear line around the angle of the building. This drew attention toward the entrance to the amusement park behind.

3.2 Dreamland Cinema front (illuminated), 1934. A surface pattern of parallel horizontal lines, repeated in the setting of the publicity signs, further balanced the vertical fin. In daylight these signs stood out against the dark recesses, while at night they were silhouetted against illuminated backgrounds, echoing German techniques.

The architects commissioned to design the new cinema were Julian Leathart and his partner W.F. Granger, whose previous work on London cinemas had caught the attention of architectural critics.[31] Between 1926 and 1930, the partnership completed seven cinema commissions that reflect a range of influences from Ancient Egypt (Kensington, 1926 and Beaconsfield, 1927)[32] to vernacular Spain (Twickenham, 1928 and Richmond, 1929).[33] Leathart and Granger's penultimate cinema, however, represents a dramatic departure from earlier work. The Sheen Kinema, East Sheen (1930), clothed a relatively modest interior in full-blown art deco garb. The façade was primarily influenced by continental precedents, signalling a break with the American atmospheric and Granada style. Its façade featured the dramatically imposing centrepiece of a double-height vertical bay window and neon sign. The influences visible in The Sheen, with its emphasis on night-time lighting (a German speciality), found full expression at Dreamland.

Leathart and Granger's new cinema complex at Dreamland was extensive, comprising (in addition to the 2,200-seater cinema) a 1,500-capacity ballroom, and restaurants and dining halls holding up to 3,500 diners.[34] The scheme, which began in late October 1933, was designed to be carried out in stages, with the cafés and restaurants opening first in the summer of 1934, and the cinema being built in just six months between September 1934 and March the following year.

The project presented Leathart and Granger with a series of structural and planning problems. The original ballroom had to be accommodated within the framework of the new scheme, and the site was on particularly unstable ground. This necessitated pile foundations of reinforced concrete, and the use of light building materials, such as cellular bricks.[35] The approach road to the amusement park at the rear was preserved by raising the cinema auditorium by 12 feet to allow traffic to pass underneath.[36]

The architects' solutions for the various technical problems dictated the layout of the complex, yet their final scheme represents a highly original and effective meeting of the site's requirements. Their attention to the structural needs of the building was matched by their understanding of its function as a place of commercial entertainment. As Leathart reflected in 1935, the Dreamland Cinema front was 'an attempt to reconcile the necessity for large areas of advertising display on the main façade facing the sea with the preservation of some architectural character and dignity.'[37]

The principal feature of this façade is an 'audacious soaring fin tower', with 'Dreamland' in coloured neon lettering running down each side.[38] This defining feature can be seen as the culmination of Leathart and Granger's attempts to develop a new style, foreshadowed at The Sheen, and reveals an admiration for German Modernism. In adopting German models, Leathart and Granger created a building which itself functioned as publicity for Dreamland (see Figures 3.1 and 3.2).

On entering the main elevated doorway, the visitor was faced with a long entrance hall, leading to a top-lit circular cinema entrance hall and box office. A seam of internal staircases connected the cinema to the Sunshine Café above, and the bars, shops and restaurants below. Although each component of the complex was directly accessible from the street, these staircases allowed the visitor to circulate around the whole building and its facilities without stepping outside.[39]

The unusually long entrance hall, with the cinema foyer so far back from the main entrance, not only channelled visitor movement through the building in an orderly fashion, it also created a sense of transition from the noise and chaos of the street to the suspended reality of the cinema. This sense of other-worldliness was further enhanced by the simple but luxurious decoration.

The finished Cinema won praise from both Margate's residents and the national architectural press; *The Architects' Journal* of 1934 featured Dreamland alongside Lubetkin's Penguin Pool at London Zoo, and other pioneering buildings.[40] While each element of the cinema was highly functional in its own right, Leathart and Granger maintained the overall coherence of the design, rendering the whole scheme greater than the sum of its parts. This distinctive formula became associated with the Odeon façades after Cecil Clavering and Harry Weedon successfully adapted the idea for the Odeon circuit.[41]

A Modernist dream?

Leathart and Granger's use of German models should be viewed in the context of a body of work by British architects in this period who were inspired by continental Modernism. During the late 1920s, Berlin saw

3.3 Titania Palast, Berlin (Ernst Schöffler, Carlo Schloenbach and Carl Jacobi, 1928). This cinema, and others like it, became a model of night architecture for British architects employing backlighting and neon bands to define the form of the building and its advertised attractions.

a series of cinema projects that became icons of Modernism. The UFA Universum, designed by Eric Mendelsohn (1928), used functionalism to create a 'machine for viewing'. Its curved horseshoe exterior, reflecting the shape of the auditorium, was dissected by a rectangular tower marking the entrance, and supporting a neon sign. The composition of the Universum is clearly echoed by Leathart and Granger, and in turn became a talisman for the Odeon exteriors.[42]

German buildings such as these pioneered the use of self-advertisement as an architectural virtue.[43] The German architects used lettering and display as an integral part of the design, rather than appearing as an ill-coordinated afterthought (see Figure 3.3).[44] P. Morton Shand's polemical *The Architecture of Pleasure: Modern Theatres and Cinema* (1930) called for such examples to be followed in Britain: 'Night architecture is [a] type of modern design with immense possibilities for beautifying our cities ... Publicity lighting is becoming to architecture what captions and lay-outs are to journalism.'[45]

What then, were the ideological implications of the debt to German Modernism at Dreamland? As a regular contributor to various architectural journals, Leathart was clearly well aware of the progress of Modernism in Britain and on the Continent, particularly after the influx of acclaimed German Modernists in 1934, such as Gropius, Breuer and Mendelsohn. Yet, while he admired the work of such individuals, it cannot be assumed that Leathart's adoption of a European Modernist style at Dreamland signifies any ideological empathy with the movement. In their purest forms, the Modernist buildings of, for example, Wells Coates or Lubetkin, embody a number of recurrent themes, such as egalitarianism, internationalism and collectivism, but evidence of social and political discourses at Dreamland are more difficult to locate.

At first glance, the strong German influence and clear similarities with Mendelsohn's work suggest that Leathart was positioning himself along similar ideological lines. Leathart certainly took his social role as architect very seriously. His book, *Style in Architecture* (1940) is essentially a defence of modern architecture in which he condemns traditionalism and ornamentation, and upholds the use of reinforced concrete and steel-framed structures. Buildings should, he maintained, reflect and adapt to modern life.[46]

In his view, the relationship between society and architecture is crucial, yet his commitment to Modernist architecture is based on technical rather than ideological principles. Throughout the book he refuses to be drawn into a discussion of political or cultural ideals. For Leathart, it seems, Modernism was more about new materials and engineering achievement than about social utopianism.

Leathart's commitment to the Modernist style was shared by Dreamland's owner, John Henry Iles, but perhaps for different reasons. The Cinema's opening brochure sums up the mass-appeal policy of Dreamland as 'The bringing of happiness to the many at a price they can afford'.[47] If the Modernist cinema had associations of egalitarianism, it suited Iles's commercial concerns very well. Iles's main priority, however, was that the new building substantiate promotional claims of novelty, that Dreamland was a *modern* complex of a calibre equal to any. As the opening brochure asserted, the reconstruction of the seafront block made Dreamland 'one of the finest and most comprehensive entertainment centres in the kingdom'.[48]

Moreover, the impetus to modernise the Dreamland complex was intensified by the work of architect Joseph Emberton at Blackpool Pleasure Beach in the early 1930s. Emberton's major redesign was a powerful endorsement of Modernism, promoting it as a suitable replacement for the exotic Coney-esque architecture that had dominated seaside resorts until the 1920s. His iconic 1939 Casino, for example, which replaced the original 1913 Indian Palace building, had a circular central form with a wide expanse of glass, tipped by a circular white tower. Stripped of all traditional decoration, the 'pleasure' function of the building was expressed through a concrete corkscrew, which flagged the entrance to the Pleasure Beach.[49] Iles shared Emberton's desire to increase the number of middle-class clientele at Dreamland, and his view of modernisation as 'clearing-up, of putting order into chaos'.[50]

Though European Modernism often provoked fierce debate among professionals and the general public in Britain, it featured heavily in the mainstream architectural press, and perhaps this potential for pre-opening publicity also appealed to Iles. Indeed, the featuring of Dreamland in so many of the contemporary journals suggests a very effective self-promotion strategy.[51] Furthermore, the preference for German models may be attributed to the fact that, by providing eye-catching self-promotion during the day and after dark, they fitted Dreamland's requirements most closely, and contrasted dramatically with the other cinemas in Margate at the time. The use of the new rational architecture at Dreamland made sound commercial sense.

Viewed in this context, the Dreamland Cinema complex was not about ethics, but rather about image. In a sense, Dreamland can be seen as a metaphor for the Modernist Movement in Britain as a whole, which generally operated not as an ideological force for change and social progress, but as a set of fantasies. Through exposure to the new aesthetic in fashion magazines and advertising, the 'modern look' became associated with affluence and with progressivism in taste, but not necessarily politics.[52] British film audiences, exposed to the Modernist sets of glossy Hollywood films such as Edmund Goulding's *Grand Hotel* (1932) and William Cameron Menzies's *Things To Come*

(1936), now found these cinematic visions solidified in the exteriors of the new cinemas. In this way, as an extension of the fantasy world of the movies, the Odeon cinemas' style inaugurated at Dreamland was not so different to that of the atmospherics they transcended, once the latest novelty but by 1935 denounced as 'pandering to mass vulgarity'.[53] Both attempted to attract their audiences by capitalising on the latest associations of exotic and intriguing lifestyles or, as Donald Albrecht put it, the 'modern mystique'.[54]

The amusement park: contextualising the cinema

To understand the implications of the new complex at Margate, its relationship with the rest of Dreamland is crucial. The cinema represents the fruition of Iles's long-term development strategy for the site as a whole. In recreating Dreamland as a bastion of modernity, Leathart and Granger, by implication, would also transform the amusement park behind, or so it was hoped. Novelty was the key. Fresh attractions raised visitor numbers and profits, and amusement parks all over Britain vied for pre-eminence by increasing their turnover of rides.

While the new cinema complex functioned as a self-contained unit of entertainment, it was also carefully conceived as the frontage of the amusement park. The entrance to the park is, in effect, a giant portal, through which the visitors passed. A brightly lit tunnel, which ran underneath the auditorium, funnelled the crowds into the park, where they were met by the noise and bustle of the fairground. Despite the formality of the façade, the new cinema scheme contributed to the atmosphere of excitement and otherworldliness.

Certain parallels can be drawn between the experiences of being in the cinema complex and of being in the park behind. The cinema building and the amusement park provided the opportunity of suspending the reality of everyday life, of briefly casting off the limitations of routine and work. Both offered an escape from the chaos of the street and beach outside: the new complex with its calming interiors and sedate Sunshine Café (see Figure 3.4), the park with its ornamental gardens and zoo. Both provided simulated experiences of some kind: the cinema audience absorbed in the love scene or the daring escape, the roller coaster, safely locked to its rails, with its passengers screaming

3.4 Sunshine Café, Dreamland Cinema, 1934.

in fear. The visitor to the amusement park and the cinema paid to experience anticipation, suspense and mirth.

While the technologies of the roller coaster and the film projector might be seen to be in direct competition at Dreamland, I would suggest that in offering a similar experience of liminality, their coexistence was highly productive.[55] The connection between cinema and mechanical rides is well established. Moving pictures first became accessible to a wider audience when they were taken up by travelling fairs as the latest novelty. The fairground served to popularise film between its rudimentary beginnings and the first generation of permanent cinemas in the early 1900s, and it was in this context that the first conceptual crossover between mechanical thrill rides and the cinema occurred.[56]

In 1906 Hale's 'Tours' appeared in England, an enterprise imported from America in which travelogue films were projected in a mock railway coach – made to sway like a real train, giving the sensation of a ride through the Swiss Alps, or the Rocky Mountains. The Tour even included a uniformed ticket collector equipped with a flag and whistle. The concept was franchised, and Tours appeared around the country, surviving in London and Birmingham until 1912.[57] In the context of the fairground novelty ride, the distinction between the mechanical ride and the cinema was extremely fluid.

A connection can be made between the taste for fast-action films, which seems to characterise working-class Londoners' tastes in the 1930s, and the thrill of ersatz danger experienced in an amusement park such as Dreamland.[58] Like riding a roller coaster, watching the daring stunts of Harold Lloyd or the fast-paced slapstick misfortunes of the Keystone Cops, was an 'edge-of-the-seat' experience, in which the audience was safe in the knowledge that no real risk was being taken. Such films depicted technology out of control, speeding cars, runaway trains, perilously high skyscrapers and escapes made in the nick of time. The most successful roller coasters of the 1930s manipulated similar themes, incorporating hidden turns and precarious drops at break-neck speed, before delivering the riders safely back to the loading bay.

At Dreamland, both the cinema and the park were essentially conceived as 'total' experiences, which aimed to cater for all tastes within one complex. The circulation of the cinema interior, like the amusement park itself, was designed to contain visitors, to keep them amused for the whole day, thereby maximising consumption.

Conclusions

Ultimately, the new cinema represented an attempt both to modernise and to refine Dreamland's image. To achieve this, Iles turned to European models of mass entertainment, rejecting the more whimsical Coney Island aesthetic that had impressed him twenty years before. Aspiring to capture a wealthier class of visitor, Iles commissioned a complex he hoped would be worthy of both the casual day-tripper, and of the longer-stay holidaymaker. Meanwhile, the revamped amusement park continued to attract the crowds and, in fact, the mainstay of Dreamland's business came from the mass groups of workers who descended on Margate for their annual 'beanie'. That Leathart and Granger incorporated the existing Garden Café, marked on the original cinema plans as 'Beanfeast Hall', together with the provision of restaurant seats in the main complex for 3,500, is evidence of the profitability of appealing to traditional working-class cultures. Despite its sophisticated, cosmopolitan veneer, the plush new supercinema was still very much catering for the masses.

The cinema made Dreamland a highly competitive leisure provider of national repute. The glossy new front lent it an air of pioneering yet respectable modernity, which elevated it from its unrefined seaside amusement park associations. The inter-war period was Dreamland's 'golden age', and the opening of the cinema marked in many ways the pinnacle of Dreamland's success.

By combining the tenets of modernity and leisure for all, Dreamland captured the spirit of the times, and the imagination of both the architectural profession and the general public. Its future seemed guaranteed. Only four years later, however, the situation looked very different. In February 1938, Iles was declared bankrupt and relinquished control of Dreamland. The following year, the complex was requisitioned by the Government, and used to manufacture camouflage material and store military vehicles. When it reopened in 1946, Dreamland faced a society whose tastes and expectations of leisure had been profoundly altered.

Notes

1 Dreamland Cinema was awarded a Grade II* listing on 25 April 2008.

2 A discussion of the entire Dreamland complex may be read in J. Kane, 'Mechanical Dreams: The Construction of a Modern Pleasure Complex. Dreamland, Margate, 1920–1960' (MA dissertation, RCA/V&A History of Design, 2002). Lindsay Anderson's 1953 documentary *O Dreamland* shows the amusement park in action.

3 The term 'supercinema' refers to a generation of cinemas built after 1929, identified by their elaborate design, capacities of several thousand, theatre stages, and luxury bars, cafés and restaurants. D. Atwell, *Cathedrals of the Movies: A History of British Cinemas and Their Audiences* (London: The Architectural Press, 1980), pp. 87, 119.

4 S. Glynn and A. Booth, *Modern Britain: An Economic and Social History* (London: Routledge, 1996), pp. 53–67.

5 The Real Gross Domestic Product in 1920 was 108, by 1930 it had risen to 119, and by 1940, 158. *The Economist Pocket Britain in Figures* (London: H. Hamilton in association with The Economist, 1995), p. 50.

6 Glynn and Booth, *Modern Britain*, pp. 28–9.

7 The 1938 Holidays With Pay Act standardised paid holiday arrangements across the industries, and represented a government endorsement of leisure for the masses. See J.A.R. Pimlott, *The Englishman's Holiday: A Social History* (London: Faber, 1946), pp. 215–25. Also G. Cross, *Worktowners at Blackpool: Mass-Observation and Popular Leisure in the 1930s* (London: Routledge, 1990), p. 8.

8 Cross, *Worktowners*, p. 11. Although the Mass Observers were not overtly critical of the proletariat, this language illustrates their contemporary perception of the working classes as mainly passive and unsophisticated in their tastes.

9 J.B. Priestley, *English Journey* (London: W. Heinemann, in association with V. Gollancz, 1934), pp. 267–8.

10 D. Scurrell, F. Stafford and J. Whyman, *Margate 1736–1986: A Resort Guide* (Thanet District Council, 1986), p. 61.

11 A. Kay, *Tourism and Holiday Making in Thanet*, Thanet Libraries Project Pack, Margate Local Studies Centre, p. 33.

12 R. Dolling, 'Meet Me Tonight at Dreamland', *Theatrephile* 1(3), June 1984, p. 34.

13 Ibid.

14 'In Dreamland with Ritchie Calder', *Daily Herald* (14 August 1934), p. 13.

15 *Souvenir of the Opening of the New Dreamland Cinema* (Margate: 1935), accessed at Margate Museum Archive.

16 Quoted by J. Richards, *The Age of the Dream Palace: Cinema and Society in Britain 1930–1939* (London: Routledge & Kegan Paul, 1984), p. 11.

17 Ibid. The population of Britain stabilised at 40 million during the 1930s, which indicates that in 1939, going to the cinema was on average a twice-weekly event. www.statistics.gov.uk/learningzone (accessed January 2002).

18 Quoted in Richards, *Age of the Dream Palace*, p. 11.

19 Ibid., p. 18.

20 Ibid., p. 23.

21 Ibid., p. 19.

22 Ibid., pp. 20–1.

23 R. Gray, *Cinemas in Britain: One Hundred Years of Cinema Architecture* (London: Lund Humphries, 1996), p. 75.

24 Robert Atkinson's influential Regent cinema in Brighton (1921) brought the opulence of American movie 'palaces' to Britain. Gray, *Cinemas in Britain*, p. 42.

25 Gray, *Cinemas in Britain*, p. 92.

26 According to a manager of one 'select' cinema, his audiences liked 'good British films' such as Hitchcock's *The Thirty-Nine Steps* (1935). *World Film News* 1(9), December 1936, pp. 3–4, quoted by Richards, *Age of the Dream Palace*, p. 29. *World Film News* 1(11), February 1937, pp. 6–7, quoted by Richards, p. 25.

27 T. Bennett, 'Hegemony, Ideology, Pleasure: Blackpool', in T. Bennett, C. Mercer and J. Woollacott (eds), *Popular Culture and Social Relations* (Milton Keynes: Open University Press, 1986), pp. 135–54.

28 Ibid., p. 144.

29 See Bertrand Russell's optimistic *In Praise of Leisure* (1935), and Henry Durant's *The Problem of Leisure* (1938). Cross, *Worktowners*, p. 7.

30 Richards, *Age of the Dream Palace*, p. 12; M. Tapsell, *Memories of Kent Cinemas* (Croydon: Plateway Press, 1987), pp. 81–3.

31 Leathart had the more prominent career of the partnership. His reputation as an architectural critic is confirmed by his contribution to an edition of *The Architects' Journal* devoted to cinema design. See J.R. Leathart, 'Structure and Facing', *The Architects' Journal*, 7 November 1935, 667–72.

32 J. Hutchinson, *A Dream Came True* (Margate: by the author, 1995), pp. 30–1. *Architect and Building News* (11 November 1927), p. 749.

33 Gray, *Cinemas in Britain*, p. 60; Atwell, *Cathedrals of the Movies*, p. 80; Hutchinson, *A Dream Came True*, p. 31.

34 Hutchinson, *A Dream Came True*, p. 45.

35 *Building* (June 1934), p. 207.

36 Leathart, 'Structure and Facing', *Architects' Review* (7 November 1935), p. 668.

37 *Sight and Sound* (May 1935), p. 13, quoted by Hutchinson, *A Dream Came True*, p. 36.

38 Gray, *Cinemas in Britain*, p. 93.

39 The use of centrally positioned staircases to provide complete interior circulation, and the light and airy interior is comparable to that of the De La Warr Pavilion at Bexhill (Mendelsohn and Chermayeff, 1935).

40 *Architects' Journal* (June 1934).

41 Clavering was inspired by the early publicity about Dreamland to incorporate vertical fins in the much-imitated Odeon façade at Kingstanding, Birmingham (1935), and at the Sutton Coldfield, Scarborough and Colwyn Bay cinemas the following year. Gray, *Cinemas in Britain*, pp. 92–3.

42 Ibid., p. 81.

43 See J. Ward, *Weimar Surfaces: Urban Visual Culture in 1920s Germany* (London: University of California Press, 2001), p. 111.

44 Gray, *Cinemas in Britain*, p. 82.

45 P.M. Shand, *The Architecture of Pleasure: Modern Theatres and Cinemas* (London: B.T. Batsford, 1930), p. 28.

46 See J. Leathart, *Style in Architecture* (London: Thomas Nelson, 1940), p. 19.

47 *Souvenir of the Opening of the New Dreamland Cinema* (1935).

48 Ibid.

49 S. Braggs and D. Harris, *Sun, Fun and Crowds: Seaside Holidays Between the Wars* (Stroud: Tempus, 2000), p. 6.

50 Cross, *Worktowners*, p. 98.

51 In addition to *The Architects' Journal*, Dreamland was featured by *Architecture Illustrated* (June 1934), pp. 190–7; *Architect and Building News* (15 June 1934), pp. 311–16, (5 April 1935), pp. 12–15; and *Building* (June 1934), pp. 204–11.

52 D. Albrecht, *Designing Dreams: Modern Architecture in the Movies* (London: Thames & Hudson, 1986), p. xii.

53 S. Bernstein, *Architects' Journal* (November 7, 1935), p. 657.

54 Albrecht, *Designing Dreams*, p. 110.

55 Literally meaning threshold, 'betwixt and between', here the term 'liminality' refers to the ambiguity of the ritual realm, where everyday reality is transformed into a symbolic experience which thereafter affects the individual's lived-in reality. See V. Turner, *The Ritual Process: Structure and Anti-structure* (Harmondsworth: Penguin, 1974).

56 Gray, *Cinemas in Britain*, p. 12.

57 Ibid.; also D. Robinson, *World Cinema: A Short History* (London: Eyre Methuen, 1973), p. 33.

58 In 1936, Richard Carr reported that 'East End audiences … like good pictures, good American pictures, pictures of movement and action', *World Film News*, 1(11), February 1937, pp. 66–7, quoted by Richards, *The Age of the Dream Palace*, p. 25.

4 ✧ Worlds in a box: technology and culture in 1950s British radio design

David Attwood

I very much remember my dear Roberts radio.[1]

DESPITE SIGNIFICANT TECHNOLOGICAL DEVELOPMENTS, in particular the solid-state transistor device, the aesthetic of the British radio set in the 1950s and early 1960s was above all socially shaped. Drawing heavily on the consumer study carried out via the *Radio Times* in 1994, which surveyed two hundred consumers who bought or used a radio in the 1950s, this chapter combines the analysis of extensive 'popular memory' material with wider research into the design, production and retailing of radio sets in the post-war era. It looks at why people bought radios in the 1950s and considers how they went about choosing them and how they were then used. Above all, it explores what people's radios meant to them and suggests that as television displaced radio as the prime provider of family-centred domestic entertainment, the growing economic and cultural independence of young consumers brought about a key shift in the radio set's significance.

The starting point for this project was a request placed in the listings magazine *Radio Times* in September 1994. Approximately 250 replies were received, many providing vivid perspectives on radio both as a functional means of consuming programmes and, on a more symbolic level, as an expression of modernity or a treasured and fondly remembered 'possession' or 'companion'. Following a preliminary analysis of the responses and personal interviews with five selected respondents, a questionnaire was designed and sent to fifty-five others.

This set out to analyse purchase and usage patterns for different types of radio more systematically, and assess levels of agreement with specific attitude statements.[2]

The sampling method used has undeniable shortcomings, particularly in terms of class, as those who responded were self-selected from among those with the motivation and fluency to do so. Accuracy of recall after some forty years, and the effect of the 'nostalgia' factor must also be taken into account. However, selection for the follow-up survey was balanced as far as possible in terms of respondents' gender and location, while the survey included a question on employment (at the time the radio was obtained) as an approximate indicator of economic and social status.

These concerns were also addressed by considering material from other sources. Studies carried out in the late 1940s by the pioneering social-survey group Mass Observation provided additional evidence of listening habits and attitudes to radio.[3] Reference was also made to an exhibition-linked study from 1990, *Putting On The Style*, which set out to establish how people living in London furnished their homes in the 1950s, using written and oral testimonies.[4] This research (though touching only briefly on radio ownership and use) provided useful insight into the preferences of social groups (such as council tenants and people living in poor-quality rented accommodation) who were probably under-represented in the primary material. Overall, the research provided an unexpectedly rich, if incomplete, perspective on the emotional responses of consumers to radio ownership during the post-war period.

The radio as status symbol

The 1950s saw an increasing understanding by the British radio industry of American marketing techniques, such as annual fashion-based model changes and the use of superficial differences to create distinctive products within a range. Retailers, too, were moving with the times, with more accessible displays of merchandise; a 1955 radio-trade journal advised them to 'let the customers maul the goods … if they touch them enough they get attached and a sale is made'.[5] With functional performance increasingly taken for granted, retailers focused on the fashion or furniture values of radios as much as their technological merits; one 1958 guide advised that 'when asked "which is the best set?" the salesman should reply "there is no such thing ... if I were you, I'd simply take the one with the cabinet your wife likes best".'[6]

Excitement and pleasure in owning a radio for the first time was widely expressed in the *Radio Times* survey. One man stated that wirelesses were among his own 'first real possessions', while a female respondent remembers being given one for her twenty-first birthday, thinking 'it was one of the greatest inventions ever'.[7]

For newly married couples or those starting work, a radio was often a high priority, and frequently seems to have been a symbolic acquisition marking a new life and a new status: 'It was the first thing I bought at a few shillings a week when I first started work at 15',[8] and 'We established ourselves in a furnished flat ... we had little money ... nevertheless we *had* to have a radio'.[9]

In furnished accommodation a radio could be particularly important, as the *Putting On The Style* research suggests: 'in a drab room, having a gramophone, a radio or a television could make all the difference, and for many tenants these were high priorities'.[10] On the other hand, there were also disincentives to ownership: landlords sometimes charged tenants extra for owning and playing a radio, while immigrants familiar with jukeboxes and American broadcasting were disappointed by the programme choice (predominantly BBC) and, like teenagers later in the decade, were more likely to buy record players. The high cost of a radio, particularly the first transistor models, as a proportion of income was frequently expressed in the *Radio Times* data. A set bought in 1956/57 'cost £23, which was more than a week's joint income for us in those days'.[11] As one woman recalled: 'From our wedding present money of £150 my husband and I bought a Bush pushbutton radio. It cost eighteen guineas [£18.90]. This was in 1950. The £150 was supposed to be the basis of a deposit on a house and our elders were shocked at this extravagance.'[12] A radio as a *possession* could evoke powerful emotions, especially for women: 'a present from my husband on my birthday ... I loved it dearly',[13] and 'For many years it was my constant companion on the kitchen windowsill ... its demise was like the loss of a trusted friend'.[14]

4.1 Radio advertisement, early 1950s

Several writers have shown how the ideologies encoded in 1950s advertisements for domestic appliances and office equipment defined women's duties and ambitions at home and at work.[15] Advertisements of the period aimed at encouraging women to purchase their own radios played powerfully on images of increased leisure, freedom and travel, and such preoccupations took on a physical form in sets that adopted a 'luggage' aesthetic of fabric-covered wood (see Figure 4.1).[16] Some women at least appear to have engaged with these images, even if the actual goods were inaccessible: one wrote of a radio which 'looked like a minute attaché case … and was the first of its kind I had seen. However it was priced at £24 and much too extravagant'.[17] Another recalled that she 'expected to spend time in France and thought it would withstand the rigours of travel'.[18] Even if actual travel was not envisaged, there were always the exotic possibilities conjured up by the theoretically receivable foreign stations often marked on tuning dials at the time; as another wrote: 'There were wonderful names on the dial – I never have found out where Hilversum is'.[19]

The lure of modernity

By the late 1940s wartime communications requirements had made many components smaller and more efficient, and this in turn made compact self-contained radio sets practicable. From the mid-1950s, the printed circuit technique also made sets lighter and easier to mass-produce. Then, in the five years after 1956, the solid-state transistor replaced the larger and more delicate glass radio valve. By 1960, portable transistor radios were a hugely successful consumer product.[20] One respondent quoted from a letter she had written in 1958: 'I have bought a tiny portable radio with transistors instead of valves. It's just terrific.'[21] Newness and novelty of presentation were powerful drivers to purchase; one man chose a Murphy table model 'because it looked a new design and exciting'; for another respondent her boyfriend chose a set 'for its novelty and convenience at a time when portable radios were large and cumbersome'.[22] And indeed a review of the 1957 London Radio Show noted that 'a novelty now gaining respectability is small-scale radio, with tiny medium wave sets using printed circuits and transistors instead of valves.'[23] 'Respectability' here carries the sense that tiny radios were no longer to be seen as toys or gimmicks: an enduring stigma noted by other radio historians.[24]

When radio became a personal accessory, this modernity seemed to attach itself to the owner. One man wrote 'I can remember thinking how modern and up to date I felt.'[25] Visible status was all-important: one woman recalled that a transistor radio was 'something of a status symbol among my fellow students ... I remember my first transistor radio with affection ... It brought fun and relaxation into our lives'.[26] In fact, the transistor epitomised modernity even more powerfully than mere portability did; as a 1959 trade review confirmed, 'the transistor has a glamour about it that will revive lively interest among the free-spending young people for all types of portable generally'.[27] But the component's very invisibility necessitated a highly visible statement of its existence, as one respondent described her radio: 'ALL TRANSISTOR (the words are writ large on the front!)'[28] For, as the cultural commentator Reyner Banham would note in 1963: 'Pop design ... exists to be seen and ... to reflect splendour on its owner. The mere possession of a far-out transistor set ... adds inches to the height, much as possession of a loaded gun does in a Western. This Colt 45 quality is very appropriate to small equipment such as transistors which ride around on the person.'[29]

Elegant surfaces

As well as new internal technologies, new cabinet materials were available to radio-set manufacturers. While pre-war materials, such as veneered plywood or Bakelite, were still used for table models, new plastics such as cellulose acetate and polystyrene gave designers greater freedom to experiment with the colour and shape of smaller sets.

An elegant new radio was a major purchase, given pride of place in the home. One woman recalled: 'We bought a lovely cream Bakelite one ... we hadn't even got anything to put it on in the dining room, but having a lovely mahogany block floor ... it rested on that.[30] And another described the purchase of an 'elegant mahogany-cased model with push-button controls – not unlike the ivory keys on a piano'.[31] The description of the radio as a symbol of luxury is worth noting here. Push-buttons were promoted as a rational ergonomic simplification, but, as *Design* noted in 1957, were in fact 'a sound psychological touch; a bit of art, a hint of creative talent and status combined like a piano in the front parlour, and right up to the minute by saving one second in ten once an evening'.[32]

By contrast, the modernity of plastics was sometimes less desirable: 'A Bakelite cabinet looked cheap and nasty, but the wooden veneered cabinet was also a piece of furniture'.[33] This may be seen as an emotive rejection of a material seen as cheap, or as symbolic of unwelcome cultural changes, but, as the next section shows, more rational explanations for avoiding plastic were often given, especially by male respondents.[34] Like other consumer products of the period, a particular model would often be available in a number of 'fashion shades', and, especially where a radio was a personal purchase rather than for family use, the colour could be a significant issue. A portable bought almost 40 years earlier was recalled by one woman in the sensuous detail appropriate to a fashion accessory as finished in 'oatmeal and dark green suede finish leatherette'.[35] Another wanted 'a radio to match our decor so it was pale green Bakelite'.[36]

These were in fact the final years of a distinctive and diverse radio industry in Britain. A series of trade agreements from 1958 gave the go-ahead for large-scale imports of transistor radios from Japan, and by 1962 nearly half the sets on the market were imported.[37] Such products generally adopted styling idioms from the USA, their main marketplace, and foreshadowed a more or less uniform international style in consumer electronic products in subsequent decades.

Gendered choices: radio and the domestic aesthetic

One male respondent who recalled choosing a set because 'it suited our Ercol furniture and looked more homely'[38] appears an exception, as 'homeliness' was not the kind of attribute often cited by men. If appearance could not be justified on rational grounds, men tended to choose status-enhancing words like 'smart' and 'handsome'.

For men, radios, like cars, were seen as products that they were expected to 'know about'. Fluency with technological data, even where not strictly relevant to the purchasing decision, was far greater among male respondents. A rational modernity is often apparent: 'we opted for this model since the BBC was claiming that VHF radio was the thing of the future'.[39] For men, even aesthetic decisions are usually linked to performance: 'We chose [it] because we believed that the traditional wooden box provided a better quality of sound'.[40] Another man chose a similar set 'on technical specification and performance (with my wife's approval of its appearance).'[41] The trade, too, felt that women were less likely to care about performance; one journal remarking in 1955 that 'small, pretty sets can still get along without VHF'.[42]

In fact, the introduction of both VHF broadcasting and the long-playing record in the 1950s stimulated a new genre of technologically sophisticated 'high fidelity' equipment purchased mainly by men. Radiograms (though drawing on basically similar technologies) were valued by women for their furniture-like attributes: one typically was 'a nice piece of furniture and our pride and joy, at the time'.[43] The growth of hi-fi (though a minority market) highlighted the tensions between a male hobby and women's ideas of domestic harmony and interior design.

Meanwhile, some purchasers, usually those betraying 'contemporary' preferences, went to considerable lengths to match their radio with their decor:

> Around 1952 [my parents] had just redecorated the lounge, doing one wall very daringly in the new 'contemporary' paper – yellow with glasses and spiky coffee tables all over it. The radio was a light wood and my Mum thought it looked very modern sitting on the green painted cabinet in the corner.[44]

Such respondents could afford to decorate from scratch, and therefore had the opportunity to experiment with new styles. For others, existing furnishings tended to dictate the appearance of acquired objects (and thus were often a conservatising force in design terms). But for some consumers with limited resources, a radio or TV could be, as design historian Scott Oram has suggested, a way of 'penetrating "the modern" in an inexpensive and if necessary piecemeal way'.[45]

Portability and personalisation

Carrying a radio around could still be an unfamiliar concept in the 1950s; one man wrote that 'an unusual feature was a carrying handle on top for taking it from room to room', and a woman that a new set 'accompanied me to every room in the house – a great novelty'.[46] The survey showed that table radios were more likely to be used mainly in the living room (or equivalent), and less likely to be used in the kitchen or bedroom. Portable sets, whether valve or transistor, were much more likely to be used mainly in the bedroom, but only the transistor portable appears to have penetrated the kitchen significantly.[47] Having one's own radio in one's own space was highly prized; as one woman noted: 'It was a real luxury to have my own radio in my bedroom.'[48]

In fact, the larger portables of the early 1950s were rarely carried about in the way their design and their advertising might suggest (see Figure 4.1); one woman remembered 'buying myself a portable radio which was ... quite large and heavy really (it was the batteries that made it heavy, they weighed a ton)'.[49] But one man noted that size and weight were not always a barrier to portability: 'It was a rexine-covered suitcase about 15 x 8 x 5 inches ... it was used daily, both at home and on outings, for over ten years.[50]

With the small 'personal' portables of the period we can see the distant precursor of the Sony Walkman and iPod audio players. One man wrote, 'I did a lot of cycling ... I could listen on an earpiece while riding along'.[51] Short battery life was a greater problem with valve portables than their size and weight; one man mentioned that 'it cost a fortune in batteries'[52] and another that 'I could not afford to run it'.[53] In fact, the research suggests that sets with a mains or battery option were rarely used on batteries, and low running cost, at least as much as their small size, was the main selling point of transistor radios for some years after their introduction: 'it was nothing short of miraculous to have a small radio which ran on torch batteries that lasted for months'.[54]

The listening audience fragments

In a 1947 Mass Observation survey, 'How people spend their Saturday night', the response 'radio/sitting with family' was more often given by men than by women.[55] This might suggest that while listening to the radio (and perhaps operating or adjusting it) was seen as an active pastime for men in the evenings, it was a more passive experience for women, who might be doing something else while listening, and possibly have less control over the set.

However, when in 1949 Mass Observation investigated the radio-listening habits of households in two British cities, it found that in most households and 'under almost all circumstances' women were the main radio listeners.[56] Two-thirds of weekday listening took place in the evenings, though 15 per cent of households were found to keep their wireless sets 'tuned in' for most of the day. On Sundays, however, nearly half the households kept their sets on for most of the day. 'Indiscriminate radio listening' increased with 'lowering of social status' and 'amongst larger families'. What is rather dismissively described as the 'habit' of listening to the pop music station Radio Luxembourg was 'strongest amongst working-class households'.[57]

4.2 Advertisement showing a family listening to a radio, 1947.

The class and gender-based assumptions behind this survey are revealing. The author of the report comments that 'it is, of course, inevitable that on weekdays radio listening will mostly be confined to the evenings'; keeping the radio on most of the time (which on

4.3 Early 1960s livingroom with the radio as focal point.

weekdays housewives and children at home would of course have been
more likely to be able to do) is dismissed as 'indiscriminate listening'.

How did people use radios, alone or together, and where? These
questions are inextricably linked with the practicalities of portability,
changing family circumstances and cultural preferences, and the coming
of television. In the late 1940s, the radio was still the main source of
home entertainment: a typical advertisement of the period showed a
family clustered round a radio listening to a 'frightening' radio play,[58]
while a later photograph shows a radio still occupying the focal point
which would soon be taken by a television set (see Figures 4.2 and 4.3).
At this time, as one woman commented, radio was a binding force: 'a
member of the family on solemn or joyous occasions ... people stopped
to listen'.[59]

Away from the domestic sphere, radio could be a means of connecting with it or replacing it; one man recalled that 'a radio was essential [during National Service] since it relieved home sickness ... knowing that folks at home were listening to ... the same programmes.'[60] But radio ownership was still unusual outside the family home, and in these circumstances communal listening persisted into the mid-1950s: 'Very few students had radios in those days and many a time my room was crammed as we listened to *Saturday Night Theatre*'.[61] And one respondent who was at university in 1955 remembered 'I was very popular as it was the only radio in my corridor. Many a slice of toast was burnt listening to *The Goon Show*, or the Top Twenty on Radio Luxembourg'.[62]

Television and the teenager

By the mid-1950s, however, the TV set was becoming the physical and cultural focus in many living rooms. With radio's role increasingly relegated to the provision of music and news, listening patterns fragmented as family members started listening individually in different rooms around the house. Radio manufacturers quite soon identified this trend as a means of selling more radios and launched 'second sets', many of which were styled (often in rather stereotypical ways) to appeal to men or women (see Figure 4.4). Family members listened alone or together depending on the time of day, and certain programmes were linked to this, as the BBC increasingly scheduled programmes to align with the routines of housework, work and school:

> My father's main use for the radio was ... listening to the news. My mother always listened to *Mrs Dale's Diary* and as a family we always listened to *The Archers, Have A Go, Educating Archie, Journey into Space* and Saturday night plays ... Like my schoolmates, I was an avid listener to *Hancock's Half Hour, The Goon Show* and Radio Luxembourg.[63]

As a radio became older, or family circumstances changed, its role within the family could change, from individual to communal use, or vice versa; one woman bought a radio and 'had it alongside my bed ... [later it] was moved to the kitchen mantelpiece'.[64] Another recalled that 'in 1959 a television set came to supplant the wireless, which went to live in my bedroom'.[65] As this response suggests, the advent of television

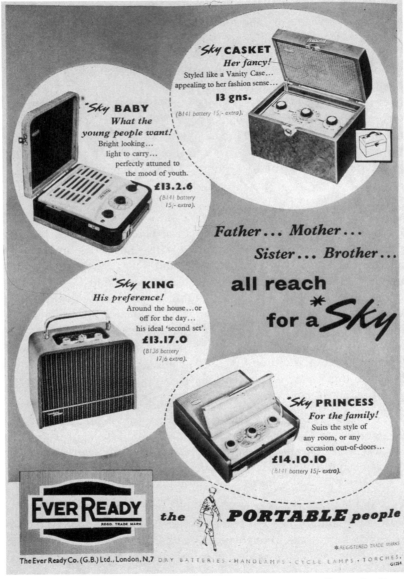

4.4 Advertisement for radios in cabinets styled to appeal to different family members, 1950s.

as a family focal point made the shared experience of listening less usual. The survey showed that television affected radio listening considerably, and this is authenticated by BBC listening figures.[66] One said: 'After we got TV we listened to radio a lot less, except father who listened on his own in his "music room".'[67] The new hi-fi phenomenon has already been mentioned, and here we see the male reclamation of listening space, which it either required or permitted. Keir Keightley has suggested that post-war trends, such as the move toward smaller, open-plan homes and the onset of family TV viewing, compelled some men to establish separate hi-fi rooms as a way of reclaiming their own space and escaping domesticity.[68]

This male separateness soon became a generational one. There was a strong age factor in the fragmentation of the listening audience as, with the growth of rock and roll and pop music, teenagers began to need their own space and their own radio. The increasing affluence of teenagers (and indeed the invention of the word as a defining demographic term) marked them out as a valuable market for radio manufacturers.[69] As discussed below, radio's appeal for many British teenagers was limited by the programming policies of the BBC, but this only helped to romanticise the alternative sources of pop – Radio Luxembourg and (in the 1960s) the offshore 'pirate' radio stations – and the act of listening outside the domestic sphere.

As already noted, portability meant that radio could be taken from one space to another, and this might be not only on grounds of programme preference, but also to express a symbolic separateness. One man recalled that he 'used to take the set into the "best" front room to listen to *The Goon Show*, as my parents didn't share my enthusiasm. It was cold in the winter, but worthwhile for the sense of teenage rebellion'.[70]

Changing cultures could indeed lead to generational conflict, and the retail trade had noted by the late 1950s how 'TV drives young folk out of the family circle' in search of less family-centred entertainment: 'Jazz is one reason. The older folk don't want it, and, to keep the peace, the youngsters invest in a portable and listen in another room'.[71] In the early 1950s, young people had little disposable income, but later in the decade, teenagers shared in the general affluence and developed their own subculture. As Reyner Banham noted:

Telly culture had produced a mental atmosphere so intolerably stuffy that teenagers were driven to go out. But having gone out they had to give their lives outside the home some shape, some style ... a visual style that teenagers [could] afford to turn into fairly large lumps of hardware.[72]

Older people also tended to see radio listening as a strictly private activity. One wrote: 'in those days it was socially unacceptable to play radios loud. People did not walk through the streets with them on'.[73] Thus the public listening which portability made possible was at first remarkable, as this man noted: 'I bought [an early transistor radio] just before going on holiday. I can well remember sitting on the sea front, listening to a test match on my earphone. I was the object of some attention. People at first thought I was deaf and had some new, brightly coloured hearing aid';[74] and then, with the advent of pop music, unstoppably fashionable: 'I used to take it [a large portable] on holiday and thought I was the cat's whiskers dancing on the beach to it.'[75]

The power of pop

The BBC had a monopoly on British radio broadcasting and, apart from Radio Luxembourg and certain other hard-to-receive continental stations, the 1950s listener had a limited choice of three BBC services, none of which broadcast much pop music.[76] The BBC was well aware of the twin threats to its radio-audience figures from television and Radio Luxembourg, but, like much of the establishment, had a bias against American musical genres such as rock and roll. This was not simply a matter of cultural prejudice; it was powerfully backed by the protectionism of the record companies and musicians' unions. In 1957, for example, the Songwriters Guild warned the BBC against 'spilling out' American pop music 'to the semi-Americanised "teenage" listener who, in these times of high wages and full employment, has an excess of pocket money to spend upon foolish, often vulgar, musical fads'.[77] Severe restrictions limited the number of records the BBC could play.

Luxembourg, the American Forces Network (and, later, the pirate stations such as Radio Caroline) had a powerful significance for young listeners: 'stretching out my hand every few minutes ... to keep it on station for blissfully exciting Radio Luxembourg'[78] and 'We were disappointed when the radio would not receive Radio Caroline ... Late at night under the bedclothes with an earpiece ... we used to listen to Radio Luxembourg – very daring'.[79] Though falling outside the decade under consideration, the pop pirates are significant because they became, as the *New Statesman* noted at the time, 'an integral part of the teenage way of life, a symbol of their separatism, like their clothes and haircuts'.[80] Their slick American style showed that teenage consumption of BBC radio in the late 1950s had been limited by not only the unappealing musical content but also the old-fashioned image of the presenters. Although the pirates were closed down by legislation in 1967, their effect was far-reaching in determining how British radio programming was produced and consumed subsequently.[81]

The transistor as signifier

One male respondent wrote: 'it was worth it. 208 [Radio Luxembourg] under the bedclothes, [or] annoying passengers on bus and train'.[82] But by the early 1960s, transistor radios had moved on from the personal rebellion suggested by this and other survey responses, to acquire a disreputable image in the public domain. Indeed, by then it was not difficult to find the very word 'transistor' either celebrated or condemned for what it signified. Reyner Banham noted 'the contrast between the 21-inch telly and the transistor on the beach': both had high status value, but one was 'epitomised by the impregnable uncut-moquette fastnesses of the three-piece suite ... [the other by] the swivel stools at the Wimpy-bar counter, seats that have to be ridden like a bike'.[83]

In the summer of 1961, an editorial in the *Daily Telegraph*, headlined 'Transistor Nuisance', was quick to link the new technology with moral and aesthetic decline: 'The dismal fact is that this form of personal indulgence is so widespread that few seaside authorities are likely to risk driving away transistor-addicted visitors to our resorts ... a heavy price to pay for our "civilised society".'[84] And while the 1961 song 'He just couldn't resist her with her pocket transistor' (by the British pop star Alma Cogan) clearly appropriated the word 'transistor' for its alliterative qualities rather than as a genuine symbol of feminine allure, the word's symbolic power was more acutely observed in the new TV soap opera *Coronation Street*. One episode featured a teenager walking past, flashily dressed and with a radio playing on her arm like a small handbag. Two young women look on, half envious, half critical:

> The daft little beggar! She's still at school! She's jailbait, that's what she is.
> She don't look like a schoolkid to me.
> You're dead right. Wish I were her size.
> You can tell she weren't born yesterday either. Just look at the state of her, with her transistor radio! [85]

Thus, for a few years at the start of the 1960s, the 'transistor' was not only a symbol of technological modernity, but also convenient shorthand for teenage rebellion and even sexual liberation. The growing cultural and economic power of young consumers had allowed them to succeed, where gendered styling had earlier failed, in bringing about a genuine shift in the radio set's meaning.

Notes

1 *Radio Times* survey, September 1994, written testimony Female 185. Unless otherwise indicated, all quotes are from written responses to the appeal described here. The list of respondents, and the structured survey questionnaire, are included in appendices to D. Attwood, 'Worlds in a Box: Technology and Culture in 1950s Radio Design' (MPhil Dissertation, RCA/V&A History of Design, 1996).

2 For example, 'it was a "status symbol" because not many people had one like it'; 'it was something of your own, rather than the whole family's'.

3 Mass Observation reports studied included *How People Spend their Saturday Night* (1947); *Proposed Price Reductions of Radio Sets* (1949); *Radio Listening and Attitudes to Re-diffusion* [a cable radio service] (1949) and *Television* (1949).

4 S. MacDonald and J. Porter, *Putting on the Style: Setting up Home in the 1950s* (London, 1990). The study was linked to an exhibition (at the Geffrye Museum, London) of five different rooms: a living room in a 1950s council flat, a newly-weds' bedroom in their family home in a Victorian terrace, an architect's drawing room in a refurbished Regency terrace, a Caribbean immigrant's 'bed-sit' in a large privately rented house, and a dining room in a 1930s suburban home. It drew upon the memories of about 200 people who supplied written information in response to a press appeal or participated in oral history projects.

5   *Electrical and Radio Trader* (15 October 1955), p. 40.

6   *Electrical and Radio Trader* (12 June 1958), p. 43.

7   Written testimony Male 72 and written testimony F195.

8   Written testimony M44.

9   Written testimony F62.

10 'Room at the Top', in MacDonald and Porter, *Putting on the Style*, unpaginated.

11 Written testimony F39.

12 Written testimony F158.

13 Written testimony F168.

14 Written testimony F107.

15 See for example P. Sparke, *As Long as it's Pink: The Sexual Politics of Taste* (London: Pandora, 1995), p. 168, and E. Lupton, *Mechanical Brides: Women and Machines from Home to Office* (New York: Cooper-Hewitt Museum, 1993), p. 15. Such studies warn against seeing women as passive consumers of commodities encoded with patriarchal ideologies, instead suggesting that women could celebrate femininity by taking pleasure in consumption.

16 G. McCracken discusses the evocative power of products, especially those coveted but not yet owned, to act as bridges to hopes and ideals, as vehicles of 'displaced meaning'. G. McCracken, *Culture and Consumption* (Bloomington: Indiana University Press, 1988), p. 104.

17 Written testimony F68.

18 Written testimony F144.

19 Written testimony F166.

20 These developments are discussed in more detail in Attwood 'Worlds in a Box' (reference 1). See also, for example, K. Geddes, *The Setmakers* (London: BREMA, 1991).

21 Written testimony F100.

22 In trade terms a 'table model' was generally box-shaped and of such a size that it could be placed on a side table, sideboard, etc. The rear of the cabinet was usually left unfinished. Table models could vary in size, but there was an implication that they would be used in one location for most of the time, as distinct from a portable or personal set. Written testimony M151 and written testimony F127.

23 *The Observer* (1 September 1957).

24 See for example M.B. Schiffer, *The Portable Radio in American Life* (Tucson, AZ: Arizona University Press, 1991), p. 168.

25 Written testimony M61.

26 Written testimony F110.

27 *Electrical and Radio Trader* (28 February 1959), p. 6.

28 Written testimony F40.

29 R. Banham, 'A Flourish of Symbols', *Observer* (17 November 1963), p. 21.

30 Written testimony F149.

31 Written testimony F62.

32 *Design*, February 1957, p. 18.

33 Written testimony M224.

34 Sometimes a transistor radio was sold in two versions: a standard version in a plastic cabinet, and a 'deluxe' version in a wooden cabinet. Claire Catterall links post-war consumer British rejection of plastics to its cultural association with unwelcome Americanisation. See 'Perceptions of Plastics: A Study of Plastics in Britain 1945–1956', in P. Sparke (ed.), *The Plastics Age* (London: Victoria and Albert Museum, 1990), pp. 66–73. The 'good design' elite embraced the modernity of plastic, but distrusted American styling and selling techniques. In America itself, plastic had shifted from being a symbol of pre-war modernity to a cheap post-war substitute material. See J. Meikle: 'Plastics in the American Machine Age 1920–1950', in Sparke, pp. 40–53.

35 Written testimony F39.

36 Written testimony F55.

37 *Wireless and Electrical Trader*, 5 May 1962.

38 Written testimony M41.

39 VHF stood for Very High Frequency, a type of transmission now referred to as FM (Frequency Modulation). Written testimony M8.

40 Written testimony M56.

41 Personal interview M75.

42 *Electrical and Radio Trader* 27 August 1955, p. 82.

43 Written testimony F96.

44 Written testimony F166.

45 S. Oram, '"Common Sense Contemporary": The Ideals and Realities of the Popular Domestic Interior in the 1950s' (MA Dissertation, RCA/V&A History of Design, 1994).

46 Written testimony M135 and written testimony F37.

47 This was probably due to changes in programme consumption, as television became the main source of living-room entertainment. Few

table-radio owners had a television when they bought their radio; rather more valve-portable owners owned one and most transistor owners did.

48 Written testimony F11.

49 Written testimony F10.

50 'Rexine' was a proprietary leathercloth used as a cabinet covering in the 1950s. Written testimony M140.

51 Written testimony M50.

52 Written testimony M45.

53 Written testimony M180.

54 Written testimony F99.

55 Mass Observation Archive FR 2467, University of Sussex Library. The response was given by 10 per cent of men, and 4 per cent of women.

56 Ibid., FR 3105. This was true with the exception of Third Programme listening, which was equally divided between women and men.

57 Ibid., FR 3105.

58 Several historians have noted how in the 1930s the BBC created a powerful ideology of the 'radio hearth', setting out to build a family audience through middle-brow programming which rejected both unsustainable Reithian ideals and 'undesirable' American popular culture. See S. Frith, 'The Pleasures of the Hearth: The Making of BBC Light Entertainment', in T. Bennett et al. (eds), *Formations of Pleasure* (London: Routledge & Kegan Paul, 1983), p. 101; P. Scannell and D. Cardiff, *A Social History of British Broadcasting*, Vol. 1, *1922–39: Saving the Nation* (Oxford: Blackwell, 1991), p. 369; R. McKibbin, *Classes and Cultures: England 1918–1951* (Oxford: Oxford University Press, 1998), pp. 457–76.

59 Written testimony F76.

60 Written testimony M180.

61 Written testimony F68.

62 Written testimony M135.

63 Written testimony M167.

64 Written testimony F122.

65 Written testimony F166.

66 A comprehensive account of the organisational and socio-cultural switch from sound to vision is available in Vol. 4 (1945–55) and Vol. 5 (1955–75) of A. Briggs, *A History of Broadcasting in the United Kingdom* (Oxford: Oxford University Press, 1995). On this point see Vol. 4, p. 511.

67 Personal interview F76.

68 K. Keightley, '"Turn it Down!" She Shrieked: Gender, Domestic Space and High Fidelity 1948–59', in *Popular Music* 15(2) (Cambridge, 1996).

69 M. Abrams, *The Teenage Consumer* (London Press Exchange, 1959) was an influential market report on this topic.

70 Written testimony M66.

71 *Electrical and Radio Trade* (21 September 1957), p. 41; *Electrical and Radio Trade* (28 April 1956), p. 33.

72 Banham, 'A Flourish of Symbols', p. 21.

73 Written testimony M/F41.

74 Written testimony M25.

75 Written testimony F10.

76 The pattern of the BBC's 1950s programming was essentially that established after the end of the Second World War. The Home Service was seen as the core BBC service, with a mix of news, talks, drama and panel games. The Light Programme was a lighter blend of entertainment and music, while the Third Programme offered an ambitious output of serious music and discussion.

77 Briggs, *A History of Broadcasting*, Vol. 4, p. 691.

78 Written testimony F166.

79 Written testimony M1.

80 *New Statesman* (10 December 1965).

81 J. Tunstall, *The Media in Britain* (London: Constable, 1983), p. 45.

82 Written testimony M111.

83 Banham, 'A Flourish of Symbols', p. 21.

84 *Daily Telegraph* leader (13 July 1961).

85 *Coronation Street*, Granada TV, transmitted 17 April 1963.

II

DESIGN AND POPULAR ENTERTAINMENT: SOFTWARE

5 ✧ Design and the dream factory in Britain

Christopher Frayling

ALTHOUGH MUCH HAS BEEN WRITTEN about the role of design in the British economy and society, and about the place of design in public policy, surprising as it may seem, nothing of much consequence has been written about the image of the designer in British cinema.[1] There has been a book on modern architecture in the movies, one on the image of the fine artist especially in fiction film and documentary (Charlton Heston complaining to his besotted patrons about his back problems in the Sistine Chapel and Kirk Douglas being attacked by crows in a wheat field) and two important articles and a book on the image of the scientist in mainstream films, but the designer has for some reason been left queuing outside.[2] Work on the scientist has shown how fictional scientists tend on the whole to be lunatics, or alcoholics, or psychopaths, or obsessives of some description – I suppose Drs Frankenstein, Faustus, Jekyll and Strangelove are the prime examples – while real-life scientists in films tend on the whole to be impossibly saintly, incredibly generous, unbelievably humanitarian, and very often martyrs to their research as well – I suppose Edward G. Robinson as Dr Ehrlich, the Nobel Prize-winner who discovered a cure for syphilis in *Dr Ehrlich's Magic Bullet*, Greer Garson as Marie Curie in *Madame Curie*, Don Ameche as Alexander Graham Bell, and Spencer Tracy as Thomas Edison are the classics. Edward G. goes out with an exhortation to the people in the front stalls to 'rid men's hearts of the diseases of hatred and greed', while Madame Curie at the very moment of her scientific discovery turns to husband Walter Pidgeon and says 'Pierre – do you mind? You look first' ('He smiles understandingly' says the script, and 'touches her arm'). But on the whole, the psychopaths have won the day. The earliest animated story films, made by Georges Méliès in the first decade of this century, featured explorers and scientists as manic, top-hatted music-hall turns, belonging to something Méliès called the Institute of Incoherent Geography. Since then, it's been estimated that mad scientists or their creators have been the villains of 31 per cent of all horror or fantasy movies worldwide, that scientific or psychiatric research has produced 40 per cent of the threats in all horror and fantasy movies, and – by contrast – that scientists have only been the heroes of 11 per cent of horror movies. Equally, one could produce a chart of utopian visions of the technological future in science-fiction films, versus dystopian visions – and the dystopias, the gloomy ones, would outnumber the others by a factor of about ninety to one: from *Metropolis* in the 1920s, to *Fahrenheit 451* in the 1960s to *Clockwork Orange* in the 1970s to *Bladerunner* in the 1980s.

Do these stereotypes of 'saint and sinner' fit the image of the British designer in British films? Well, British cinema has certainly produced its share of professional saints and professional martyrs in this area. Professional saints such as William Friese-Greene played by Robert Donat, the hero of the film industry's contribution to the Festival of Britain in 1951, called *The Magic Box*. In this film, Friese-Greene was – inaccurately but understandably perhaps in the circumstances – depicted as the sole designer of cinematography and the moving-picture camera, and his struggles to persuade most of the notable British actors and actresses of the early 1950s – all working for half fees, including Laurence Olivier as the local policeman who sees the very first moving pictures – made up the bulk of the story. Here was the great British designer, being let down by less far-sighted and more worldly colleagues before winning the moral victory and the judgement of history. Incidentally, the film – which was originally intended to be part of the Festival itself – was completed some months after the Festival had closed, and it was far too wholesome to become a popular hit. Or professional martyrs such as Thomas Andrews, the designer of the White Star Liner *Titanic*, who was played by Michael Goodliffe in the 1958 film *A Night to Remember*. In his biography, by fellow Ulsterman Shan Bullock, Andrews is described – just before the great ship goes down – as 'standing alone in the smoking room, his arms folded over his breast and the lifebelt lying on a table near him. The steward asked him 'Aren't you going to have a try for it, Mr Andrews?' He never answered or moved, just stood there 'like one stunned'.[3] This directly inspired one of the most memorable sequences of the film, with the added details of creaking wood panels, ashtrays falling off tables, the motionless Andrews standing in front of an oil painting of New York harbour – called symbolically enough, *The Approach to the New World* – and most telling touch of all, consulting his stopwatch, because as designer of the bulkheads he knows exactly when the Titanic will finally sink, in a matter of minutes.

One could perhaps add *The King's Stamp*, a short documentary directed by William Coldstream in 1935 for the GPO and starring Barnett Freedman as the designer of the King George V Silver Jubilee Stamp. The opening section of the film begins with the design commission itself – accompanied by the music of Benjamin Britten – and ends with the commissioning agent saying, in sepulchral tones, 'the printer will probably have some suggestions to make'. In between, we see Barnett Freedman having a 'Eureka!' experience in the back of a London taxi. A somewhat idealised view of the design process, as indeed is the whole tradition of saints and martyrs.

But, interestingly, there have been fewer of the sinners in British cinema – and none who even approach the charisma or terrible beauty of Dr Rotwang, robot-designer in Fritz Lang's *Metropolis*, or Sebastian, replicant-designer in Ridley Scott's *Bladerunner*. What there *have* been is a series of British feature films which have attempted in various ways to show designers at work – and the issues of the day they have sometimes had to confront. I want to take four such 'moments' in British cinema, and one in British advertising, and explore exactly what public images of designers and designing emerge from them. The five 'moments' are in 1936, 1942, 1951, 1964 and 1987/88. The four films and the commercials I'll be looking at are William Cameron Menzies and H.G. Wells's *Things to Come*, which includes a vision of what life will be like in Everytown by the year 2036; Leslie Howard's *The First of the Few*, a dramatised account of the life and work of R.J. Mitchell, the designer of the Spitfire; Alexander Mackendrick's Ealing comedy, *The Man in the White Suit*, which shows the dire consequences of having a good design idea in 1951 Britain; Guy Hamilton's *Goldfinger* – which turned

5.1 The underground piazza of Everytown, 2036, from the film *Things to Come* (directed by William Cameron Menzies for London Films, 1936).

the equipment officer of the British intelligence services, known as Q, into something of a cult figure; and assorted television advertisements of the late 1980s, which created an image of the 'young designer' to suit what was then being called the design and retail boom.

First, the mid-1930s, when film producer Alexander Korda commissioned H.G. Wells to write a science-fiction epic based on *The Shape of Things to Come* (really a work of social philosophy), which not only would be the very first British epic of this kind, it would dramatise some key debates of the moment: modernism versus traditionalism, a celebration of technology and its possibilities, old-fashioned liberalism versus new-style planning and socialism, London in 1936 versus Everytown in 2036 [4] (see Figure 5.1). It would have a big budget, some £300,000. And, unusually (especially in Britain), it would present a positive view of the future and the benefits to be gained from technology, a utopia rather than the usual dystopia. The design heroes would be missionaries for Modernism. The trouble was, Wells had never written for the cinema before. Here – as an example – is a brief extract from the original story treatment, which came to light only a few years ago. It describes the building of Everytown, after the aerial bombing of the 30-year Second World War (remember, this was written in 1934). The bombing begins in 1936, followed in the 1960s by the wandering sickness and the renaissance of feudalism, then, eventually, Everytown 2036, the city of engineers and designers:

> A triumphant musical sequence ... a sequence of creative work and power. Flashes to give a crescendo of strenuous creative activity ... work in furnaces, upon embankments, in mines, upon great plantations. Men working in laboratories. This will have to be drawn from contemporary stuff, but that stuff must be *futurised* by putting unfamiliar flying machines in the air, projecting giant machines in the foreground, making great discs and curved forms swing and rotate enigmatically before the spectator. Emphasise by banners, streamers and inscriptions:

> Research
> Invention
> World Planning and
> Scientific Control

> There is a progressive improvement in ... the neatness and vigour of the
> machinery as the series goes through.

The problem facing producer Alexander Korda, director William
Cameron Menzies (himself a designer by training – he was to be
credited as the first production designer in film history, with *Gone
With the Wind* shortly afterward), and designer Vincent Korda, the
producer's brother, was how on earth to visualise all this, while at
the same time remaining true to the spirit of modernism which was
woven into the fabric of the story like a synthetic fibre. Part of the
answer arrived in the form of Bauhaus teacher Laszlo Moholy-Nagy,
who was living in London from summer 1935 to summer 1937, on
the run from the Nazis. He was added to the *Things to Come* team
in November 1935, to contribute visual ideas to this key sequence
showing the reconstruction of Everytown. H.G. Wells himself had
originally approached Fernand Léger, but was unimpressed by the
resulting preliminary drawings. Then Le Corbusier had been asked,
but politely declined, saying that he thought the people living in the
city were far too old-fashioned and preachy, and in any case he didn't
like underground cities. In the end, although Moholy contributed a few
ideas – bent glass tubing, some light displays, a helmeted diver behind
corrugated glass – the resulting architecture of Everytown was derived
by Vincent Korda from Corbusier's *Vers une architecture* (royalty-free,
one presumes) and Norman Bel Geddes's *Horizons*, and the see-through
plastic or rhodoid furniture was based on items from the latest Heal's
catalogue. H.G. Wells had ordered that 'ultra skyscrapers' were out, and
that Everytown shouldn't look like New York, or like New York looked
in *Metropolis*. He disliked the mixture in *Metropolis* of skyscrapers, a
stratified society and Biblical mysticism. What he got, instead, was
a mixture of Moholy Nagy's photographic experiments, Corbusier's
garden city, Norman Bel Geddes's vehicle designs, Vincent Korda's
streamlined *moderne* reference material from the latest magazines and
Arthur Bliss's emphatic music – all of which were intended to illustrate,
in a riot of masculine imagery, the words of the great scientific
modernist of the story and Great Air Dictator John Cabal (played by
Raymond Massey in a wide-shouldered samurai outfit): 'to tear out the
wealth of this planet, and exploit all these giant possibilities ... that
have been squandered hitherto upon war and senseless competition'.

The sequence begins with giant machines tearing out an underground site, then shows more advanced machines constructing the city of the future out of prefabricated parts. It ends with a debate about the merits of progress, during which the question is put: 'Is the world any jollier than it used to be?' Well, when H.G. Wells first saw the sequence, in a screening room at Denham studios, he turned to Alexander Korda and said 'very good machines, *but* the machines of the future will make no noise!' The sequence, he added, should have been silent. Which was strange, since he wanted the rest of the film to be so very talkative. Not least the final moments, where the debate between moderniser and traditionalist was filmed head-on – in a series of lengthy speeches about human potentiality – and conducted with a full-blown chorus scored by Arthur Bliss of the phrase 'Which shall it be?' The brotherhood of efficiency and the freemasonry of science – as H.G. Wells called them – are the clear winners. Which shall it be? Science, design, technology and planning.

Things to Come was a success in Britain – largely, it was said, because of the prophecies it contained at a time of great public interest – and it was reissued during the Blitz, when its sequences of aerial bombardment had particular poignancy. But in America it flopped. As one distributor there put it 'Nobody is going to believe that the world will be saved by a bunch of people with British accents'. George Orwell was to be even more scathing about *Things to Come* than that distributor. In 1941, he wrote in an essay 'Much of what [H.G.] Wells has imagined and worked for is physically there in Nazi Germany. The order, the planning, the state encouragement of science [and engineering], the steel, the concrete, the aeroplanes – all there, but in the service of ideas appropriate to the Stone Age'.

For our purposes, though, the point is that the image of the designer is one of a clean-cut, assured, technocratic man with a mission: the mission of modernism. This coincided exactly with government reports for design reform, art schools taking their design responsibilities more seriously and increased investment in research, design and development.

George Orwell's comment brings me neatly to my second 'moment', when actor Leslie Howard had returned from a successful career in Hollywood (most recently as Ashley Wilkes in *Gone With the Wind*,

a character he rightly reckoned was 'a fearful drip'), to make films
in support of the British war effort. His most successful film as both
actor and director was *The First of the Few*, prepared in 1941 and
released in 1942, a film which was, surprisingly, the only feature
made during the war to concern itself with the Battle of Britain[5] (see
Figure 5.2). Flashing back from that Battle, in September 1940, it told
– through David Niven's narration – of the life of R.J. Mitchell, Reginald
Mitchell, designer of the Supermarine Spitfire: how he got the idea for
a monoplane that would fly, as he puts it in the film 'just like a bird, all
in one', how the Whitehall bureaucrats put obstacles in his way; how his
romantic idealism kept him going – through initial designs for entries
in the Schneider Trophy in the late 1920s – the Supermarine 55 and 56
– to the Spitfire in the 1930s, and how he dies – partly, it is suggested,
of overwork – at the very moment of his triumph in 1937, the very first
of the few to give his life. It was by no means a saint's life, however,
for Leslie Howard made every effort to present him as a human being
– obsessed, very difficult to live with – and took several swipes at
appeasers and tight-fisted government departments. Of course the
script, by Miles Malleson, took many liberties. The real R.J. Mitchell was
the son of a Staffordshire school teacher, who became an engineering
apprentice at the age of 17: Leslie Howard locates him within a very
different class background, as a perfectly spoken, middle-class, arty,
graduate type. A fighter pilot says at the beginning of the film 'The
Spit's an artistic job', to which Station Commander David Niven replies
'That's not surprising. It was designed by an artist'. Well, it wasn't.
There is no mention of the competition – Hawker's Hurricane, of which
considerably more took part in the Battle of Britain itself, than Spitfires.
There's no mention of Mitchell's many abortive designs, or the failed
tests: 'everybody likes it *enormously*', crows the man from Vickers early
on in the design process. And the origin of the name 'Spitfire' belongs
to the realms of poetic licence as well: 'The plane's a curious sort of
bird', says Leslie Howard clutching a china tea-cup, 'a bird that breathes
fire and spits out death and destruction – a *spitfire* bird'.

What actually happened when R.J. Mitchell heard that the Air
Ministry had called his fighter the 'Spitfire' was a rather more down-
to-earth comment: 'Just the sort of bloody silly name they *would*
choose'. But the most important aspect of *The First of the Few* (called

5.2 Leslie Howard looks at the gannets in *The First of the Few* (directed by Leslie Howard for British Aviation Pictures, 1942).

Spitfire in America), was the image of the designer it put over: donnish, boyish, sweet, a little unworldly but full of good ideas, obsessive, and a gentleman. To use a wartime word, a 'boffin', and one who likes to do his thinking alone. Not at all prickly, as the real Mitchell was said to be. Leslie Howard – in blazer and open-necked shirt, looking as preppy as can be – first gets the idea that he can improve on existing designs by looking closely at the gannets over Beachy Head. 'All in one', he says, 'wings, body, tail, and yet when *we* try we build something all stuck together with strings and struts and wires. But you wait, some day I'm going to build a plane that'll be just like a bird.'

And, of course, he does. He 'hates speeches', and public appearances, and trying to persuade resources committees in Whitehall. In his manner and dress code he is isolated from both the uniformed military and the pin-striped civil servants. But when the threat from Europe hots up – with the bombing of Guernica, Northern Spain, in April 1937 – so does his pace of work. At last the threat of aerial bombardment has sunk in. The best-known sequence in the film shows in montage the race against time to produce the prototype K5054, to the strains of William Walton's 'Spitfire Fugue'. A key player is the Scots engineer in his shirt-sleeves, who turns the drawings into reality – and in this film answers to the name of Mac. His type was to recur in several 1950s films about British aviation.

We have some interesting evidence as to how the British public reacted to this film and its various messages, for Mass Observation included it in the social survey of British cinema-going habits, which was launched in November 1943.[6] A quarter of all the cinema-going men and women surveyed listed *The First of the Few* as among their favourite films of 1942/43. Comments ranged from 'informative if Mitchell bomber [*sic*] *did* come into existence like that', 'enjoyed Leslie Howard's restrained acting' and 'Spitfire Fugue'; 'historic interest … convincing story', 'unusual' and 'Leslie Howard very fitted for the part'. Clearly, the congruence of Leslie Howard's well-known star persona and that of the designer-hero struck the public as not at all far-fetched. He 'fitted' and he was 'convincing'. The missionary for modernism had made way for an image that domesticated the designers and boffins on whom the war effort depended. Perhaps as a result the image was to have quite a shelf life.

Twelve years later, in 1955 – a time of nostalgia for wartime, when the audit of peace was showing a national decline – he was still there in the depiction of Dr Barnes Wallis, by Michael Redgrave, as a donnish, introverted, charming, single-minded and solitary genius in *The Dam Busters*. We first meet him in his cottage garden experimenting with a catapult, a tin bath full of water and some marbles. Later, he explains the theory behind his bouncing bomb to a Whitehall man by saying 'there's some evidence to suggest that at the Battle of the Nile [Nelson] dismissed the French flagship with a Yorker'. The real Barnes Wallis – who trained on the job first as a marine engineer, then in rigid airship construction before designing airframes for heavier-than-air bombers such as the Wellington – advised on the screenplay of the film as well as on its main sourcebook, Paul Brickhill's *The Dam Busters*, of 1951. Here was a chance very publicly to set the record straight about his particular research contribution, which he felt had been marginalised. So the Barnes Wallis of the film has a boyish and understated enthusiasm – much less forthright than the real person – which sharply contrasts with the power games played by everyone else. Again, *The Dam Busters* did not play well in America. One of the distributors there exactly – suspiciously exactly – echoed the reaction to *Things to Come* of nineteen years before: it would be impossible, he said, to sell a film in which 'a bunch of guys with limey accents acted as if they were saving the world'.

R.J. Mitchell and Barnes Wallis were indeed very British: the designer as boffin, and his best definition came at the beginning of a film written by Peter Ustinov in 1946 called *School for Secrets*.

> The RAF has gained a reputation during the last few years, not only for being a brilliant warlike organisation, but also for inventing a new language. Among the lesser-known words that appeared in the welter of 'prangs', 'scrambles' and 'wizards' was the word 'BOFFIN'. The RAF linguistic experts will tell you this derivation of the new word. Once upon a time, a Puffin, a bird with a mournful cry, got crossed with a Baffin, an obsolete service aircraft. Their offspring was a Boffin. This bird bursts with weird and sometimes inopportune ideas, but possesses staggering inventiveness. Its ideas, like its eggs, are conical and unbreakable. You push the unwanted ones away, and they just roll back. This is the story of a handful of BOFFINS.

The designer-boffin's very best moment of donnish understatement came in *The Dam Busters*, when the man from the ministry says to Barnes Wallis, 'Do you really think the authorities would lend you a Wellington bomber, for tests? What possible argument could I put forward to get you a Wellington?' To which the boffin replies 'Well if you told them I designed it, d'you think that might help?' Cut to Barnes Wallis in the cockpit of a Wellington.

When Michael Balcon, head of Ealing Studios, had *The First of the Few* run for him on the studio's projector, his one recorded comment was that Mitchell didn't own the copyright anyway – it belonged to the company on whose time he did the designing (an aspect not covered in the film!). In 1951, Festival of Britain year, the year of my third 'moment', Balcon was to produce a comedy with this as one of its main themes, *The Man in the White Suit*.[7] The poster was designed by St John Woods. The commissions for other Ealing posters of this period – such as the one for *Eureka Stockade* by John Minton and for *The Titfield Thunderbolt* by Edward Bawden – were often given to well-known artists and designers, and Minton was to write a hilarious article for *Ark*, the Royal College of Art's student magazine, about selling his soul to Ealing.

In 1951, there was much debate in the press about designers being out of step with public taste, and about how the fashionable word 'contemporary' was often pronounced by industrialists as 'contemptible'. *The Man In the White Suit* confronts this issue of innovation versus inertia head-on, with a story about a young designer in a Northern textile factory called Sidney Stratton (played by Alec Guinness) who develops a form of everlasting white fabric which can turn the factory into a world market leader, but which is instead ridiculed and suppressed by captains of industry, retailers and workforce alike. Alec Guinness is a more genial version of the Angry Young Men of a little later on in the decade – as one critic put it, he is 'Jimmy Porter's art-or-technical college-educated elder brother'. If Ealing comedies tended on the whole to be the regimental mascots of British cinema – there is a corner of the English mind that is forever Ealing – here was one which was definitely on the side of those who didn't like rules and regulations. Throughout the film, Stratton's bubbling-over energy and creativity are contrasted with the network of deadening vested interests that surround him. In the central sequence of the film – which is, incidentally, a parody of the equivalent sequence of *Things to Come*, and features Miles Malleson, the scriptwriter of *The First of the Few*, as the long-suffering tailor – Stratton's revolutionary new design is turned into a dazzling prototype. It starts with the tin hats of wartime ('we've got the answer, Mr. Birnley, we can go ahead now') and ends with a suit that belongs to the year of the Festival – and Alec Guinness modelling it in front of an assortment of mirrors. In between, an inspired mix of 'polymerisation' and 'radioactivity' has done the trick. Yes, he has 'got the answer' but, of course, in the purity of his research, Stratton has forgotten all about the economic and social realities of early 1950s Britain. And in particular about the top-hatted textile manufacturers who speed up the great North Road from London in their convoy of Rolls Royces. Their leader Sir John

Kierlaw (played by Ernest Theriger) may be a little shaky on his feet and a little short of breath, but when it comes to defending 'the ways things have always been done', he is unstoppable. The number plate of his Rolls is AGO 585. 'I will not stand in the way of progress', says Mr Birnley (Cecil Parker), somewhat hypocritically: but he does. In the end even he realises that the interests of industry lie elsewhere. As do all the inhabitants of the town: from company chairman right across the social board to washerwoman.

Sidney Stratton's design never does get into full production. But the new image of the designer lingers on. Still slightly unworldly, eccentric and even dotty – though no longer the donnish type. Instead he is more of an angry young inventor who leads the charge against the previous generation. But doesn't get anywhere.

My fourth 'moment' dates from the mid-1960s, a time when Lord Snowdon's Aston Martin convertible would sometimes be driven by his chauffeur to faraway places such as Prague where there was to be a Council of Industrial Design exhibition; the car would then be displayed by Lord Snowdon as 'a symbol of British excellence'. The film I have chosen is *Goldfinger*, made in 1964 [8] (see Figure 5.3). When considering the image of the designer in the 1960s, more obvious choices might perhaps have been Antonioni's *Blow Up* (with its fashionably pushy photographer), or Dick Lester's *The Knack* (with its art students painting a period room, floor to ceiling, in white) or John Schlesinger's *Darling* (which tried to take the lid off London's version of la dolce vita, and especially the fashion business). But one particular aspect of the astonishingly successful James Bond films seems to me to have presented a much stronger image of the designer – the scenes involving Major Boothroyd, or 'Q', the equipment officer of the Intelligence Service.

In the books by Ian Fleming, at least those from *Dr No* onward, Major Boothroyd of 'Q' branch had been based on a man called Geoffrey Boothroyd, an expert on handguns from Glasgow who had written to Fleming pointing out the many inaccuracies contained in earlier stories. Major Boothroyd was introduced to lecture James Bond on the finer points of weapons' design – a subject which fascinated Ian Fleming, as he admitted, far more than it ought to: 'it's what you expect' he said, 'of an adolescent mind, which I happen to possess'. He

5.3 British poster for the film *Goldfinger* (directed by Guy Hamilton for Eon Productions, 1964).

remained a minor character in the saga, almost a private joke, and in the book *Goldfinger*, of 1959, James Bond didn't even have to consult him, to be issued with his Aston Martin DB3. 'The car was from the pool' wrote Fleming.

> Bond had been offered the Aston Martin or a Jaguar 3.4. He had taken the DB3. Either of the cars would have suited his cover – but the DB3 had the advantage of ... an inconspicuous colour – battleship grey – and certain extras which might or might not come in handy. These included switches to alter the type and colour of Bond's front and rear lights ... reinforced steel bumpers, fore and aft, in case he needed a ram, a long-barrelled Colt. 45 in a trick compartment under the driver's seat, a radio pick-up tuned to receive an apparatus called the Homer, and plenty of concealed space that would fox most customs men.

So, the Aston Martin it is – rather than the tried and true 4.5 litre Bentley, with Amherst Villiers supercharger.

Comparing this passage with the equivalent sequence in the film, various changes have taken place. Major Boothroyd has turned into an important character, called 'Q', played by Desmond Llewellyn, whose stiff-backed professionalism is contrasted – in a running joke – with Bond's more laid-back attitude. 'Q' is the equipment officer and designer at the head of the Quartermaster's Branch of the Secret Service. He had made his first significant appearance in *From Russia With Love* the previous year, 1963, and from *Goldfinger* onward was to become a key player. 'Oh, do behave 007 ...', and so on. Secondly, the gadgetry issued by 'Q' to James Bond with the inevitable dry lecture on its proper uses, has moved well beyond the realms of fantasy. The inconspicuous Aston Martin DB3 of the book – with its reinforced bumpers, radio pick-up and secret compartment, the equipment of your average stock-car at Wimbledon Stadium – has turned into the highly conspicuous silver DB5 of the film, with its bullet-proof windows, revolving number-plates, transmitting device with dashboard reception – 'no, it hasn't been perfected out of years of patient research *entirely* for that purpose, 007' – oil-slick squirter, wing-mounted machine guns, protruding wheel scythe and ejector seat. Incidentally, these gadgets were all developed by Ken Adam, the film's production designer, with an Aston Martin team at the plant at Newport Pagnell. As 'Q' patiently explains them to Sean Connery, he walks past – in a deliberate touch – several other classics of British design: a parking meter, an anglepoise lamp, a mini van in the background. Clearly, this car belongs to a great tradition. As Sean Connery is lectured on this latest addition to the canon, he is – by turns – intrigued, dismissive, impressed, jokey. But, as 'Q' solemnly tells him at the fadeout of the 'explanation' scene (by now part of the formula), 'I never joke about my work ...'

In a way, 'Q' is a 1960s version of the 1940s boffin, only this time in civvy street. In another, it has been suggested, he represents the voice of Commander Ian Fleming himself. But above all, he is the designer as gadget-maker. No longer as engineer working on essential technology (as he had been in wartime): such films stopped being made in Britain, round about the end of the 1950s, when they no longer seemed credible in the age of superpowers. By the mid-1960s, characters like Barnes Wallis were only in the story to be kidnapped by the Russians in the first reel. In short, 'Q' branch doesn't make Spitfires any more: it issues schoolboy gadgets, with a touch of swinging London about them.

My fifth 'moment' dates from 1987, the year when a group of advertising agencies working for television decided that the new design culture could perhaps provide them with a visual language that would help create an aura of 'hip' or 'in-crowdery' around their products.[9] And as a result they evolved my final public image of the designer, at a time when the noun was beginning to turn into an adjective.

This is at its most extreme in three particular television ads, starting with their visual language. The first is called *Scrapyard*, and it was made by the agency Gold Greenlees Trott. It begins at a used-car dump, and shows a young man removing the seat from an old Rover car, then welding it to a piece of scaffolding. We cut to his austere, sparsely furnished apartment – the only decorations appear to be a wire sculpture of a human figure, and a girlfriend who is trying hard to look exactly like Louise Brooks in *Pandora's Box*. The young man throws his soft, colourful chair out of the window on to a rubbish dump below, and sits in his reclaimed car seat enjoying a can of lager. The caption 'Less Is More' comes up on the screen.

The second is called *Easy*, and it was made by Dorland Advertising. It shows a young man waking up on a Sunday morning, in an apartment decorated with hanging pedal cycles and assorted cult objects, an apartment which overlooks a railway junction. He makes himself some coffee – in a cafetière – and then goes to a huge 1950s fridge to get some milk for his cat. We cut to him walking under a railway bridge, along a deserted street, saying hello to a newspaper vendor, and getting his cash out of a wall-bank. The final image shows him sitting in the window of his 'Metropolitan warehouse' apartment, reading a newspaper with his presumably contented cat.

The third is called *Coping*, and it was made by K.H.B.B. advertising. Again, it shows a young man in a sparsely furnished warehouse apartment – it has an old dialling telephone, a leather sofa, assorted electric gadgets including a vertical speaker system, and outside, through the windows, we can just see some red lights flickering. He switches on the television set with his remote-control, and the set promptly blows up. 'Imagine', says the commentary spoken by American actor James Coburn, trying hard to sound like Orson Welles who used to do the voice-overs until he died, 'imagine what it would be like without music'. Then he starts reading, by the light of his bent metal, exposed-bulb, standard lamp – which promptly blows as well. 'And what would we do without the table-lamp?' – as the boy picks up a can of lager, the commentary adds, 'I think we'd *probably* manage'.

Three advertisements, from three different agencies, all of which went out on British television between autumn 1987 and spring 1988. What do they have in common? Well first of all, a sense of inner-city desolation and urban transformation. The docklands apartments look out – from a great height – over a rubbish dump, a railway junction and a red-light district respectively. Inside them, resourceful male individuals tend to live alone, or with their cat, and design their own environments out of urban waste (in the first two cases) or by getting wired in (in the third) only to discover that the wiring itself is unreliable. They are urban nomads. It is an aesthetic of salvage, of junk and of sparseness: the visual style of these ads hooks into a design craze of the moment; this, in turn, creates an impression of being hip, and explains why the ads already look like period pieces. In *Scrapyard*, it is a young man throwing out a Memphis-coloured – if not textured – chair, in favour of a chair which could have come straight out of Ron Arad's One-Off Group gallery in 1985, only we see him constructing it himself. From Memphis to Salvage, with a punch-line from Mies van der Rohe. In *Easy*, it is cult objects from the history of design – the large fridge, the electric fan, the cafetière – surrounded by more salvage, in the form of bicycles and bicycle wheels which may even be a distant homage to Marcel Duchamp. In the third, it's the latest domestic technology – a grey, flat-screen television with remote control – combined with 1970s vinyl turntable, a post-Corbusier-style leather sofa, and a Castiglione-style reading lamp. A design and style culture, a metropolitan dream – or nightmare – world (depending on whether you live upstairs or not) where young, trendy designers who reclaim their own environments feel entirely at home. All to legitimate a brand of lager, or a wall-bank.

So my fifth public image of the designer is of someone who probably graduated in the mid-1980s, who can recite passages from

Blueprint as if they are part of the liturgy, and who much prefers gentrification to modernism.

What can one conclude from these five public images of the designer?

1   The 1930s missionary for Modernism

2   The 1940s pipe-smoking boffin

3   The 1950s angry, and unworldly, young inventor

4   The 1960s maker of British gadgets

5   The late 1980s style-conscious inhabitant of the wasteland.

Well, they are all male, they are all – in one way or another – eccentric, and they are all marginal people. Mainstream people do other things for a living. In fact, these designers, with the exception of 'Q', don't seem to be earning a living in the accepted sense at all: the missionary is a Dictator, the boffin presents himself as a gentleman amateur, the angry young man does his research, secretly, in his own time, and the young 1980s designer lives on his wits by an economy of makeshifts. They don't have clients, in the accepted sense. Design is usually something they do to things, rather than something that happens in a cultural, social, legal and economic world. They are all a little bit mad, as befits geniuses without honour in their own country. All except the young designers in the ads, who are supposed to be hip. These images all tend to go 'round the edge' of what designers actually do, day to day – in order to present a character that 'fits' the mindset of the audience. In the middle of all this is the real-life professional designer – about whom all the scriptwriters and directors of the films and ads I've mentioned must reckon the public knows very little indeed; despite the best efforts of bodies such as the Council of Industrial Design and the Design Council. No country has tried harder. But perhaps too much of the effort has gone into talking among ourselves. Like all professions – except that the cinema-going public has a pretty clear idea of what doctors and lawyers and even architects actually do for a living. Even engineers, from Mac in *The First of the Few* to Scottie in *Star Trek*.

I'd like to finish on a brief moment from a film made in 1958, released in 1959. It's a moment from Alfred Hitchcock's *North by*

Northwest. Two relaxed Americans are introducing themselves to each other in the restaurant car of a train speeding from New York to the mid-west.

> *Eve Marie Saint*: 'I'm Eve Kendal, I'm 26 and unmarried. Now you know everything'.

> *Cary Grant*: 'Tell me, what do you do, besides lure men to their doom on the Twentieth Century Limited?'

> *Eve Marie Saint*: 'I'm an industrial designer'.

> *Cary Grant* (after a short pause): 'Jack Phillips, sales manager ...'

Actually she's not telling the truth. She's a spy. And nor is he. He's an advertising man whom everyone thinks is a spy. But, for a woman to say 'I'm an industrial designer' – with no further explanation, and with only the very slightest of double takes from Cary Grant – that's something inconceivable in British cinema, probably even today.

Postscript

Design and the dream factory in Britain started life as the first Paul Reilly Lecture at the Design Museum in 1993. So the advertising images of 1987–1988 were relatively recent, and were received with smiles of recognition. If the lecture had been given in 2008, which images of the British designer would have been added – as a sixth 'moment'? Wallace the engineer-inventor and his intelligent dog Gromit, who first appeared in 1990 in *A Grand Day Out* in which Wallace designs a moon rocket in his potting shed because he's run out of cheese here on earth? 'Hold tight, and think of Lancashire hot-pot'. Wallace is a peacetime boffin who seems insulated from the modern world of electronics and 'we'll write it, they'll print it' because he likes to manufacture his own products as well (see Figure 5.4). Or maybe the many British television parodies of Hollywood science fiction that have followed the success of *The Hitch Hiker's Guide to the Galaxy*? Or the revival of *Dr Who*, who originally dated from a time when British cinema had dropped films about 'beating the Americans' to concentrate instead on period horror, Victorian science fiction and an array of potting-shed inventors?

There haven't been any strong or resonant images to update the 'moments' described in this discussion. Even 'Q' has been abandoned by the James Bond films. But it is worth reflecting on a couple of contemporary images of the designer, which show that the story (in Britain) could be continued in one of two very different ways.

The first image comes from American novelist Tom Wolfe's short story *2020 AD*, published in 1984 about an England of the future following the great economic collapse of 1988, in which most of the population enacts past glories, in costume, for tourists to video them. Following 1988, Disney Enterprises have moved in with an invading force, to convert the British Isles into one big theme park, the world's leading tourist attraction. The British economy, which produces nothing any more, is the envy of all Europe for the money it makes – but at what a cost! Three-quarters of the population now live in costume, inside facsimile or restored period buildings, pre-twentieth century. There are 'Pickwicks ... bobbies, pram nannies, beadles, lamplighters, coachmen ... blacksmiths, Carnaby Streeters' and of course Victorian worthies in frock coats and stove-pipe hats. That is one contemporary image, which chimes with Wallace, Dr Who and others. The second, a forward-looking one, is of a world where computers have blurred the age-old distinctions between engineering, design and science and where many areas that once belonged exclusively to physicists and chemists have now become the preserve of designers – including electronics, the nature and properties of materials, nano-technology, turning science into product and computer science itself. A world where it is more and more difficult to conceive of science without a technical outcome, and where the advance of design and technology sometimes pushes a corresponding advance in science. A person who can navigate through such a world – the world of Hollywood films such as *The Matrix* (2001) and *Minority Report* (2002), in which our heroes use graceful body-movements to touch the multiple screens that supply them with information, and they wear couture clothes – such a person may be the designer of tomorrow, navigating information to create new structures. He, or she, is now part of the repertoire of global images. It is just that British film-makers haven't yet found a way of telling their story.

5.4 Wallace, Gromit and the 'Bun-vac 6000' mounted on an old A35 van, from *Wallace and Gromit: The Curse of the Were-Rabbit* (directed by Nick Park, 2005, for Aardman/ Wallace and Gromit Ltd).

Notes

1 This chapter was originally given as the first Paul Reilly Lecture, in honour of the pioneering head of the Design Council in the glory-days of the 1950s and 1960s, at the then recently opened Design Museum. It has been adapted for publication, but not updated except for the postscript. I thought it best to leave the material more or less as delivered.

2 See for example on 'scientists' D. Robinson, 'Scientists of the Silver Screen', *New Scientist*, 3 December 1976; S. Weart, 'The Physicist as Mad Scientist', *Physics Today*, June 1988; and A. Tudor, *Monsters and Mad Scientists* (Oxford: Basil Blackwell, 1989). On architecture, D. Albrecht, *Designing Dreams* (London: Thames & Hudson, 1987) and on artists J.A. Walker, *Art and Artists on Screen* (Manchester: Manchester University Press, 1993).

3 S.F. Bullock, *A Titanic Hero: Thomas Andrews Shipbuilder* (1912, repr. Riverside, CT: 7C's Press, 1973), p. 73.

4 L. Stover, *The Prophetic Soul* (Jefferson, London: McFarland, 1987); M. Korda, *Charmed Lives* (Middlesex: Allen Lane, 1980); T. Senter, 'Moholy-Nagy's English Photography', *Burlington Magazine*, November 1981; H.G. Wells, *Things to Come* (London, 1936) and *The Shape of Things to Come* (London, 1934); C. Frayling, *Things to Come* (London: BFI, 1995).

5 C. Coultass, *Images for Battle 1939–45* (Newark, DE: University of Delaware Press, 1989); R. Manvell, *Films and the Second World War* (London: Dent, 1974); J.H. Farmer, *Celluloid Wings* (Philadelphia: Blue Ridge Summit, 1984).

6 J. Richards and D. Sheridan (eds), *Mass Observation at the Movies* (London: Routledge & Kegan Paul, 1987), especially pp. 222–98.

7 C. Barr, *Ealing Studios* (London: Cameron and Tayleur, 1977) pp. 131–145; D. Wilson, *Projecting Britain* (London: BFI, 1982); R. Durgnat, *A Mirror for England* (London: Faber, 1971).

8 S.J. Rubin, *The James Bond Films* (Westport: Arlington House Publishers, 1981); I. Fleming, *Goldfinger* (London: Jonathan Cape, 1959).

9 I am indebted to Judith Williamson (of *De-coding Advertisements* fame), for drawing my attention to this cluster of television advertisements, and to Charlotte Borgia of *Design Week* for inspiring the conclusion.

6 ✧ Taking credit: Saul Bass, Otto Preminger and Alfred Hitchcock

Emily King

THE EARLY DECADES of the Hollywood film industry were dominated by the major studios. By the mid-twentieth century, a clutch of dominant studios known as 'the big five' were churning out film after film and showing their largely undistinguished products in circuits of affiliated theatres. Audiences were captive: with no choice at the theatres and few alternative amusements, they washed in and out of the cinemas in droves. The box-office takings of mainstream American movies reached an all-time high in the years immediately after the Second World War. At this point many American adults would have seen several movies a week.[1]

The nature of movie-going in those years was very different to that of today. Films themselves were part of a much longer programme that included newsreels, animated films and other short films. Audiences would not necessarily time their arrival at the cinema to coincide with the beginning of the programme or even the beginning of the film and would often be completely unaware of the title or subject of the main feature. Rather than being viewed as integral pieces, to an extent Hollywood films were just another element in a wall of cinematic entertainment.[2]

All this was set to change. Even as the profits of the big-five studios broke all records, a case was going through the American law courts that was to loosen their grip on the movie industry. The outcome of the Paramount Case in May 1948 was a set of anti-trust laws, which required that the production and distribution of films be entirely independent of the screening of those films.[3] These laws had serious ramifications throughout the films industry, but hit the major studios hardest of all. Where previously these studios had owned circuits of affiliated theatres and so could guarantee distribution for even the poorest of their movies, now they had to rent out their product on a film-by-film basis. No longer a by-the-yard commodity, now each picture began to be judged on its own merits.

At the same time as they were dealing with the outcome of the Paramount case, the studios were facing another challenge of an entirely different nature: television. During the 1950s televisions made their way into more and more American homes, and potential movie audiences were increasingly shunning the big screen in favour of its small-scale, stay-at-home sibling. All in all, the combined effect of anti-trust legislation and TV was a dramatic fall in the number of films made by the North American Studios. The output of the big five went from 234 to 215 in the decade 1945–1955 and had plummeted to 167 by 1966.[4]

The blockbusters of the 1950s and 1960s were big-budget efforts to drag the American public from their houses and into movie theatres. As the director Elia Kazan put it, to survive 'the triumph of television' movies must be 'good or big'.[5] Matching scale with cultural pretension (think of *Ben Hur* 1959 or *Cleopatra* 1963), most blockbusters aimed to be both. The film critic Penelope Houston pointed out that as a strategy, blockbustering was self-defeating; an industry cannot survive by producing film after film, each one intended to stand as the single movie audiences need see all year.[6] Nevertheless blockbusters continued to be made through the 1960s, and even now the film industry still seems to be experiencing a hangover of the blockbuster mindset.

Although 'big' may have been the single most significant characteristic of the film industry during this period, 'good' also played a role independent of scale. Many of the new breed of producer/directors who had found opportunities to make films after the decline of the studio system had well-developed artistic aspirations. These individuals wished to promote their own films as the output of a singular, authorial vision and believed themselves to be making a product of significant cultural worth. More than that, these film-producer/directors wished to assert their identities above those of the studios who were still involved as part-funders of most independent movie projects. In order to achieve all of these ends, some of the most ambitious film-makers of the 1950s, men such as Otto Preminger (1905–1986) and Alfred Hitchcock (1899–1980), chose to preface their films with graphically adventurous title sequences. These sequences completely overwhelmed the impact of the studio logo that audiences would have seen on the screen immediately before and also created an instantly recognisable film identity that could be carried over into posters and press campaigns.

The graphic designer employed by both Preminger and Hitchcock to create their most memorable title sequences was Saul Bass (1920–1996). Born and raised in New York, Bass had been designing publicity material for the film industry since he moved west to Los Angeles in the late 1940s.[7] Up until the mid-1950s, Bass's involvement with film had been very conventional, most of his designs being for standard-format film posters. Preminger made a bold decision to hire Bass to design animated titles for his 1955 film *The Man with the Golden Arm*. Up until that point, film titles had for the most part consisted of a filmed series of appropriately lettered placards, a style developed from the traditions of signwriting. Having no precedent within feature films, Bass's form of titling bore a stronger relationship to the animated shorts that had padded out the film programmes of the pre-war decades. As a graphic designer involved in the making of feature films, a person responsible for welding word, image and live action, Saul Bass was a pioneer.

Saul Bass has become a graphic-design and film-making legend. His name is synonymous not only with a graphically sophisticated approach to film titling but also with a graphic sensibility to film-making in general. Bass was designing title sequences right up until his death in 1996, but his reputation was sealed with the work that he undertook for Preminger and Hitchcock at the start of his film career in the late 1950s and early 1960s. The fruitfulness of Bass's early years in film was the outcome of a happy combination between an adventurous spirit in film-making on the part of Preminger and Hitchcock and an expanded field of graphic design that was the legacy of the American importation of European graphic Modernism. In order to more fully explore Bass's contribution to the film-making of Preminger and Hitchcock, the rest of this chapter will focus on two films: the aforementioned 1955 Preminger film *The Man With The Golden Arm* and Hitchcock's 1958 film *Vertigo*.

The Man with the Golden Arm

The film *The Man with the Golden Arm* was based on Nelson Algren's socialist realist novel of the same name, which was first published in 1949.[8] Starring Frank Sinatra as Frankie Machine, a man with an addiction to drugs and gambling, the film was strong meat for the 1950s American public. In the film's central scene, against a background score of chaotic, freeform jazz, Frankie Machine is shown succumbing to drugs. This was a scene made all the more shocking to 1950s audiences because of the casting of Sinatra, an actor more likely to be dealing with dance manoeuvres than needles. Compared to Algren's book, the film is coy. Preminger cleaned up the grinding poverty and degradation described by Algren so that contemporary reviewers complained the film had 'dulled the sociological backdrop'.[9] Yet, by not shirking from the book's central dilemma, that of a man dealing with a heroin addiction, Preminger created a drama that was startlingly frank.

Predictably enough *The Man with the Golden Arm* caused a great deal of controversy. In order to release the film, the distributors United Artists were required to resign from the Movie Picture Association of America (M.P.A.A.), the film industry's self-regulating body, that had refused to grant it their seal of approval.[10] Preminger, who had come up against the M.P.A.A. once before over his 1951 sex comedy *The Moon Is Blue*, welcomed the opportunity to rekindle his antagonism with the Association. Railing against their 'antiquated' production code, the director insisted that the M.P.A.A. had 'no influence on the American movie-going public'.[11] The lasting legacy of Preminger's high-profile battles against the American film industry's self-imposed censorship was a hastening of the revisions of the unimaginative moral code of the Association. The immediate effect of the director's outspokenness was to raise the profile of his own films, and some cynics have suggested that his constant thwarting of the censors may have been part of an ongoing publicity strategy.[12]

Whether Preminger was engaged in the broad battle for artistic freedom or a narrow campaign for personal notoriety, the film-maker's ambitions regarding his own product were absolutely clear: to retain control of all aspects of movie-making. Preminger was the perfect beneficiary of the changes the anti-trust laws had wrought on the industry. In his autobiography, he claimed to have been 'one of the first to take advantage of the opportunity' to produce independent films.[13] Significantly, Preminger's bid to determine the nature of his films went beyond what was normally considered to be the sphere of the producer/ director and extended into the realms of the distributor and publicist. Not only demanding the final cut of movies, he also attempted to control which posters would be used to advertise those movies. In the case of *The Man with the Golden Arm*, Preminger refused to allow theatres to show posters with an image of Frank Sinatra and only allowed those displaying the disjointed arm logo designed for the film by Bass (see Figure 6.1).[14] As with the censorship battle, Preminger's conflict with the publicists can be interpreted in two ways. Either it can be seen as the assertion of artistic integrity, the daring insistence on publicising a film using a semi-abstract graphic symbol, or as an egotistical move, an attempt to quash the identity of Frank Sinatra, a personality that would trump the celebrity of Preminger.

Overall, Preminger's bid to control the publicity of his films met with mixed success. The press books that were circulated with the British release of Preminger's movies reveal that, of the wide range of posters that were available to British cinemas, only a small proportion had much in common with the publicity material generated by the director himself. In the case of the 1957 Preminger film *Bonjour Tristesse*, Bass's teardrop logo was eliminated from the film's international publicity and replaced with a series of much more cheery images that sold *Tristesse* as a summer movie. Similarly, in the posters available for the promotion of the 1959 film *Anatomy of a Murder*, conventional montage portraits of the film's major stars were overlaid with a clumsy adaptation of the film's original Bass-designed typeface. But although Bass's title sequences were not followed through to become coherent, all-embracing graphic identities of the kind that Preminger might have hoped to create, they did amount to striking cinematic interventions.

The starting point for Saul Bass's title sequence for *The Man with the Golden Arm* was Elmer Bernstein's jazz score for the film – it was the first and last time that Bass created a sequence to synchronise with a pre-existing piece of music.[15] The sequence, like the movie, is in black and white and, for a large part of its running time (under three minutes), the screen is filled with white rectangles dancing against a

6.1 Poster for *The Man With The Golden Arm* designed by Saul Bass, 1955.

6.2 *opposite* Stills from the title sequence for *The Man With The Golden Arm*, designed by Saul Bass, 1955.

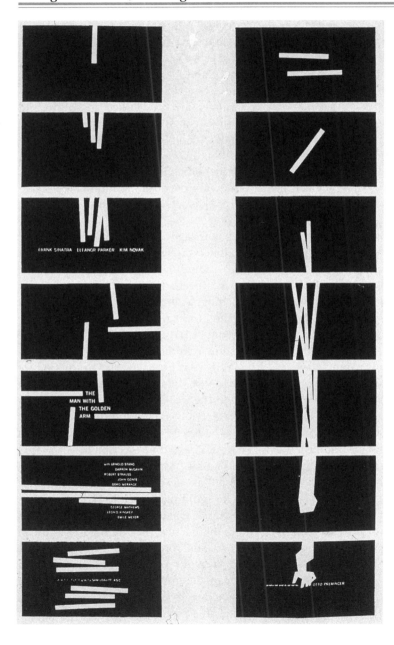

black background. Over the course of the sequence the film's credits appear as blocks of text that arrive and leave from the sides of the screen in time to the music (see Figure 6.2).

Both in its relationship to music and its formal qualities, the titles refer to the animation of the pioneer of absolute film, Oskar Fischinger (1960–1967). Unlike Bass, Fischinger always worked to music and his aim was to create a visual equivalent of auditory experience. The Fischinger films that most strongly resemble Bass's sequence for *The Man with the Golden Arm* are his 'Studies', a series produced between 1921 and 1925. In each of these cinematic pieces, abstract white forms dance against a black background in time to a well-known piece of classical music, for example Paul Dukas's *The Sorcerer's Apprentice*, and Brahm's *Hungarian Dance*.

Possibly because of their close marriage between form and familiar music, these films proved immediately accessible and were packaged to appear as short films in British movie theatres. Yet, in spite of the populist potential of his work, Fischinger's brushes with mainstream film were not happy. Famously, having helped develop the idea for Disney's *Fantasia* (1940), he left the production team in disgust at the progress of the film, unable to reconcile his artistic principles with the commercialism of the American movie industry. At their parting Walt Disney is said to have told him 'You want to make art, I'm looking for entertainment'.[16] As a result, Fischinger's ideas had their most visible impact in mainstream film through the work of Saul Bass.

In many ways it was appropriate that Bass should bring Fischinger's ideas to the mainstream. Saul Bass had been educated in the version of the Bauhaus tradition that had been adapted for American consumption by European émigrés such as Laszlo Moholy-Nagy (1895–1946) and Gyorgy Kepes (1906–2002).[17] Bass discussed graphic design in terms of 'problem-solving' and his guiding principle was that ideas should be whittled down to their essence and then relayed using the simplest possible graphic form.[18] In practice this implied the use of abstraction: simple, semi-representational forms that seemed to have an expressive and intellectual edge over their representational equivalents. Fischinger was himself a European émigré with direct links to the Bauhaus, and like Bass would have favoured the abstract, though it is likely that he would have justified this preference less in the rational terms of problem solving and more with reference to spiritual ideas derived from Eastern religions.

In spite of holding compatible ideas about graphic form, Bass and Fischinger would have parted company decidedly when it came to the issue of narrative film. Where Saul Bass had a native love of the Hollywood movie, Fischinger thought that the conventional dramatic structure of mainstream film was inappropriate to the medium and should be shrugged off in favour of the pursuit of absolute film, a term that he associated with animation. It is unlikely that Fischinger would have approved of bolting on abstract animation to a live-action feature. Bass on the other hand was very attracted to the medium of live-action film, and later in his career gave up all use of animation in favour of creating titles from tightly edited live-action sequences. By the late 1960s, animation had all but been abandoned as an adjunct to serious feature films. Barring one or two spectacular exceptions, for example Richard Williams's extraordinary animated sequences for the 1968 movie *The Charge of the Light Brigade*, it had become a technique used solely for comic purposes, such as the opening sequences for the *The Pink Panther* films. Fischinger's 'absolute film' project survived only through the work of a small group of artist film-makers known as 'the West Coast abstract school', a group that included film-makers such as Malcolm Le Grice.[19]

The centrepiece of Bass's animated titles for *The Man With The Golden Arm*, the symbol of the disjointed arm that was used right across the film's publicity, was described by Bass as a form that 'expressed the jarring disjointed existence of the drug addict'.[20] By communicating the film's theme symbolically, Bass and Preminger were implying that the film was more an allegory than a piece of specific social critique. This was significant because it separated *The Man with the Golden Arm* from realist films made in the pre-war years such as *The Grapes of Wrath*, the 1940 adaptation of John Steinbeck's novel. Where Darryl F. Zanuck, the producer of *Grapes of Wrath*, saw his movie as a 'stirring indictment of conditions which … are a disgrace and ought to be remedied',[21] Preminger promoted *The Man With The Golden Arm* as a much more generalised tale of good versus evil. This shift away from the particular discussion of social ills was characteristic of a general tendency in post-war America. Realism had become intractably associated with Europe's fascist and communist dictators, and in America a stance described by Serge Guilbaut as 'politically apolitical' was in the ascendant.[22]

There is a striking resemblance between Bass's *Golden Arm* symbol and the twisted and distorted limbs that were depicted in Picasso's painting *Guernica*. It is likely that this similarity is no coincidence. *Guernica* toured the United States in 1939, and even if Preminger and Bass had not visited the painting itself, it is unlikely that they could have avoided seeing the work in reproduction. *Guernica* was a controversial image. Whether it was accepted or rejected by mid-century American art critics seems to have hinged on whether they judged the image to be sufficiently abstract. Arguing that the painting was an attempt at the epic that had fallen into the declamatory, the prominent art critic Clement Greenberg was unimpressed. Ad Reinhardt, on the other hand, viewed the painting as a huge success, insisting that it symbolised 'cruelty and waste, not in a local spot but all over our one world'.[23] In other words, the contributions of artists like Picasso or film-makers like Preminger were deemed worthwhile only when their themes were seen as grandly universal.

Both Preminger and Bass repeatedly stressed that *The Man with the Golden Arm* was a film aimed at a 'grown-up' audience.[24] This audience was courted not only through the visual idiom of abstraction but also through the musical idiom of jazz. In mid-century America, jazz music occupied a unique position – not only popular and commercial, it was also regarded as artistically radical. By attaching a jazz score to his film, Preminger could break boundaries and make money at the same time. Sold as an independent product, inside a sleeve illustrated with the disjointed arm logo, Bernstein's *The Man with the Golden Arm* soundtrack became a best-selling record.

Bass continued to work with Preminger through the 1950s, creating graphic symbols and title sequences for a whole series of films. Between them the graphic design for these films created a distinct and sophisticated presence for Preminger movies, just the identity that the film-maker desired.

Vertigo (1958)

After working for Preminger, Bass went to work for another major player in independent film-making, Alfred Hitchcock. It is obvious why the film-maker would have been attracted to the work of the designer. Like Preminger, Hitchcock was notoriously egotistical and controlling and, again in common with his colleague, he was eager to assert ownership of his films. Throughout his career, from his earliest directorial outings in England in the mid-1920s, Hitchcock had used all vehicles of publicity available to promote himself, his films and his artistic pre-eminence. It was long before the waning power of the studios in the 1950s made way for independent film-making that Hitchcock first began to assert his own identity.[25]

In the decades before the director first worked with Bass, Hitchcock's bid for a public profile had met with a great deal of success.[26] In 1939 he signed a contract with the production company Selznick International that gave the company the power to prepare the final cut and determine post-production of any films that the director made under that agreement. In spite of this contractual clause, Selznick was happy that Hitchcock should discuss the Selznick/Hitchcock films, the most prominent of which was *Rebecca* (1940), as if they were solely a Hitchcock product. Hitchcock had developed a situation in which his authorial association with a film was a marketable asset. Rather than creating an identity for Hitchcock, Bass's task was to develop that identity into something that would signal Hitchcock's expanding cultural and artistic aspirations.

In an interview conducted by François Truffaut toward the end of the director's life, Hitchcock admitted 'the story was of less importance to [him] than the over-all visual impact on the screen'.[27] For this reason, graphic design was a tool perfectly suited to Hitchcock. Although it can be used with narrative intent, to enhance storytelling, graphic design will always serve as an interruption within the structure of a traditional narrative film. Hitchcock welcomed these sorts of interruption, and it is characteristic of his films to contain scenes that have little do with the unfolding story and everything to do with immediate cinematic impact. In spite of this appreciation of the visual impact of graphic design, Hitchcock did not share Preminger's desire to preserve the integrity of the graphic images created to promote his films. The press books that accompanied *Vertigo* show a spectrum of advertisements making free-range use of the motifs that Bass designed for the film, many of which show photographs of the director himself. In one particular image, Hitchcock seems to peer down on the spiral motifs that Bass created for the title sequence. The headline reads 'Alfred Hitchcock engulfs you in a whirlpool of terror and tension'.[28] Hitchcock was ever the showman, and his love of the visual was unrelated to the modernist-derived quest for visual coherence that inspired Preminger.

Hitchcock may have been a die-hard populist, but even so he did have significant artistic ambitions. These ambitions appear to have been boosted in the 1950s by the circle of film-makers and critics who were keen to promote the serious analysis of mainstream movies. In 1951 the magazine *Cahiers du Cinéma* was launched, introducing a set of ideas which eventually developed into a full-fledged theory, that of the auteur. This theory, first expressed formally by the American critic Andrew Sarris in the early 1960s, maintained that the value of a film lay in the qualities that could be attributed to its author – in other words, the film's director.[29] To merit the title of auteur, a film-maker's work must consistently exhibit a body of recognisable cinematic qualities. Given this criterion, Hitchcock was a prime candidate for the epithet and was canonized by the *Cahiers du Cinéma* crowd.

After being embraced by young French film-makers, Hitchcock's artistic credibility received a boost back in the United States. In the late 1950s several of Hitchcock's films were included in the collection of the Museum of Modern Art in New York. The director was probably mindful of this status and, to a certain extent, by employing Bass to work on his movies he was making them more akin to the avant garde American films that made up the bulk of the MOMA film library at the time.[30]

The title sequence for *Vertigo* falls into two parts: the first, a series of black and white, screen-filling close-ups of the actress Kim Novak's features; the second a succession of spiralling, coloured, geometrical figures through which the camera appears to dive, one after another (see Figure 6.3). The theme of the movie is uncertain identity. The male lead Scottie, played by James Stewart, attempts to foist the identity of one woman onto another, although the audience is left with a degree

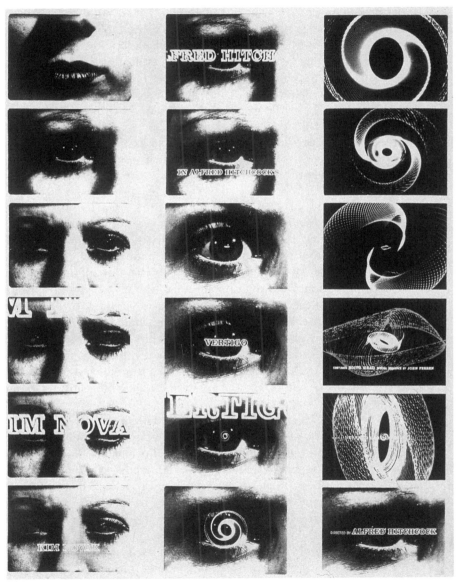

6.3 Stills from the title sequence for *Vertigo* designed by Saul Bass, 1958.

of uncertainty as to the absolute identity of either. With that theme in mind, the former section of the sequence is an examination of the most superficial sign selfhood, the face, and the latter section is a metaphor for an entanglement with deeper and more perplexing questions around the same issue. Appropriately the credits shown over the first part of the sequence, placed above a twitching lip or a shifting eye, are those for the major stars and the directors. These names – Kim Novak/James Stewart/Alfred Hitchcock – are themselves singular identities attached to well-known personalities, superficial masks of a sort. The blocks of text crediting the remainder of the leading cast and the production team appear over the second half of the sequence in a more pragmatic arrangement.

Dividing the first half of the *Vertigo* titles from the second is a short sequence in which Kim Novak's right eye, at that moment filling the entire screen, is suddenly flushed red (this moment coinciding with the chime of a bell in Bernard Herrmann's score). Then, from the pupil of the red-stained eye, the title of the film appears. Written in fairly traditional, sturdy, capital letters, the title expands, appears to move toward the audience, and then leaves via the top edge of the screen. As the title departs, it is followed immediately by the first of the geometrical figures: a round spiral that emerges from the centre of the eye grows to fill the screen and then leads the audience through the vortex at its centre. The audience has been led from the outside into the mysteries that lie within and the use of red to signal the shift leaves no doubt as to the danger implied.

The technology used to trace the geometrical figures onto the screen in the *Vertigo* sequence had been developed by the West Coast experimental film-maker John Whitney. John and his brother James were part of the small resurgence of interest in experimental film on the West Coast in the immediate post-war years. They employed mechanical means of image making, aiming to achieve a 'truer vision of reality by destroying particular representation'.[31] In the case of the *Vertigo* spirals, the technology Bass used to make these forms was adapted by Whitney from radar equipment used in the Second World War. The Whitney brothers were not the only ones to be attracted by the effect of light traced on a screen. In the early 1950s an exhibition of 'electronic abstractions', images made on the screen of a cathode-ray oscilloscope, toured several museums in the United States creating a stir among the design community.[32]

Making an association between these forms and inner mental states, Bass did not just take on the forms of the Whitney brothers, but also a chunk of their ideology. Like Fischinger before them, the Whitneys had an interest in a freewheeling set of Eastward-leaning spiritual beliefs including 'Jungian psychology, alchemy, yoga, tao, quantum physics, Krishnamurti and consciousness expanding'.[33] As such, Bass's use of Whitney's spirals to represent mental complexity was very much in line with the experimental film-makers' original vision. This association between geometrical form and psychological state was to become more and more commonplace in the decade that followed. Through those years (and, to some extent, even now) geometrical illustrations became the graphic norm of popular psychological and psychoanalytical publications, both forms of publishing that became increasingly popular over the 1960s.

The titles for *Vertigo* are not so much a distillation of the film, more an embellishment. The sequence's suggestion of a labyrinthine mental state on the part of the female lead offers the audience just one of many possible routes into the substance of the film – in some ways quite an unlikely route given the extremely passive, empty-vessel-like manner in which Kim Novak played the central Madeleine/Judy character. Contemporary critics viewed the *Vertigo* titles unimaginatively, seeing them either as an ingenious cinematic device or as a lingering look at Kim Novak's beauty.[34] Although Bass's sequence was favourably mentioned in many notices, *Vertigo* was not well received either in the press or by the public at the time of its initial release. In spite of a spiralling popular interest in inner mental states, psychology and psychoanalysis, the film failed to strike a chord among 1950s American film audiences.

Since then, among film's inner critical circles, the reputation of *Vertigo* has risen to great heights. Placed near the top of most 'best-ever' film surveys, almost always rated above any other Hitchcock film, *Vertigo* now has an assured position in the canon. Just as *Vertigo* has fared well over the years, so particular elements of the film have also been singled out for attention. In particular, Bernard Herrmann's score has also enjoyed a very successful semi–independent afterlife. Performed frequently in concert halls, the music has also been the subject of a work by the contemporary British artist Douglas Gordon.[35] In Gordon's piece, Herrmann's score is played as it is heard through the film, with gaps the same length as the unaccompanied passages of the movie. Showing only a cinematic image of a conductor's hands and face as he leads the orchestra, Douglas's piece recasts Herrmann's music as the film's major player. For those who have seen the movie, the opening passages of the film's score, the section that accompanies Bass's titles, is impossible to interpret as anything other than the sound of spirals. Coincident, but not synchronous, Bass and Herrmann created a sound and image match that, once seen, cannot be disentangled.

Bass designed the titles for three Hitchcock movies in succession: *Vertigo* (1958), *North by Northwest* (1959), and *Psycho* (1960). In the last of these films, Bass's role evolved beyond 'title designer' into 'picture consultant', a credit that reflected his involvement in the creation of the movie's celebrated shower scene. Bass's part in the shooting of this sequence was to become something of a controversy in Hitchcock's later years. Bass claimed the shower scene as his own, holding detailed storyboards as evidence. Hitchcock admitted Bass's influence in sketching out the sequence, but insisted that the designer had very little to do with committing the images to film.[36] Without going into the complexities of this, it is possible to use the episode as an illustration of the paradox involved in the employment of one person to enhance the authorial identity of another. That the communication of Hitchcock's (or Preminger's) singular authorial identity required the services of Bass creates immediate problems for the notion of cinematic authorship as a whole.

Conclusion

The rise of the title sequence in tandem with the emergence of independent film was no coincidence. As well as allowing film-makers such as Preminger and Hitchcock to assert their identities, they played other, more prosaic roles. Significantly, the mode of independent film generated much longer credit sequences. In the days of the studio system, the large part of any film's production team would have been on the studio payroll with no credit required. After the collapse of this system, these teams were hired, individual by individual, on a contract basis. It became (and remains) customary for such contracts to contain a clause about size, screen time and position of credit. By taking a more adventurous approach to movie titling, film-makers were attempting to make the new lengthy credits bearable for audiences to watch.

Yet, while credits grew longer and longer, the graphically considered title sequences of the 1950s and early 1960s all but disappeared. Reduced to the role of cinematic novelty by the late 1960s (think of Richard Williams's animated titles for *What's New Pussycat?* in 1965), they had pretty much disappeared by the 1970s (with Bond movies the only exception). Although in part the simple outcome of the tides of fashion, it seems likely that television would also have had a hand in prompting the demise of the graphic title sequence. The crammed schedules and frequent advertisement breaks that are characteristic of the small screen mean that television programmes need to be clearly signalled with distinctive title sequences. As television ownership became near universal in the US, film-makers struggled to distinguish their product from that which could be viewed at home on the small screen. By the late 1960s, graphic title sequences might have spoken too strongly of domestic entertainment rather than box-office draw.

Saul Bass's own career echoed these developments. By the mid-1960s he had begun to use live-action footage in his title sequences, a particularly successful example being the prowling cats that introduce the 1963 movie *Walk on the Wild Side*. In the early 1970s he made a film of his own, the rather extraordinary *Phase IV*. But as the 1970s progressed, Bass's film jobs became rarer, and the designer began to concentrate on his extremely successful corporate design practice, Bass/Yager Associates. It was only toward the end of his life that Bass began to work in title design again. Forming yet another close relationship with a well-known film director, Bass made titles for several Martin Scorsese films in the early 1990s, including *Cape Fear* (1991) and *The Age of Innocence* (1992). For Scorsese, employing Bass was a self-conscious revivalist step. Particularly in the case of *Cape Fear*, a remake of a 1950s movie, Bass's titles were brought in to evoke the ghostly spectre of the film's previous incarnation.

Around the same time that Bass was enjoying a late-career flourish with Scorsese, several other directors were returning to the idea of the graphic film introduction. Best known among the younger generation of film-title designers emerging around this time is Kyle Cooper. In his celebrated titles to the movie *Seven* (1995), Cooper corralled the graphic styles characteristic of the early 1990s – the digitally provoked assemblage of David Carson – into a meaningful prologue to a tale of serial killing. This sequence employs the most modish graphic language available, but even so it smacks of nostalgia. The graphically considered title sequence seems intractably bound to an imagined golden age of film, an age associated with larger-than-life impresarios like Alfred Hitchcock.

Notes

1 J. Finler, *The Hollywood Story* (London: Octopus Books, 1988), p. 34.

2 Most anecdotal evidence supports this view, for example this account from the film producer David Cammell of stealing into cinemas in the early 1950s: 'They used to have continual programmes then, they didn't stop, so I used to hang about by the exit door and when someone came out I would prop it open and sneak in.' David Cammell in interview, 21 May 2004.

3 G. Nowell-Smith (ed.), *The Oxford History of World Cinema* (Oxford: Oxford University Press, 1996), p. 445.

4 The news for the film industry was not entirely bad. The cutbacks by major studios made way for some independent movie-making concerns. The number of films made by independents rose from 143 in 1945 to 177 in 1955 and by 1966 the independents were vastly out-producing the studios with a total output of 285 films. Finler, *The Hollywood Story*, p. 280.

5 Ibid., p. 34.

6 'P. Houston, 'Blockbustering', *Sight and Sound*, Spring 1963, p. 68.

7 The following account of Saul Bass's career is drawn from an interview between the author and Bass at his Beverly Hills office on 14 July 1992.

8 N. Algren, *The Man with the Golden Arm* (New York: Doubleday, 1987).

9 *Time* (USA), 26 December 1955, p. 23.

10 *The Film Daily* (USA), 8 December 1955, p. 4.

11 Ibid.

12 Obituary of Otto Preminger, *New York Times*, 24 April 1986

13 O. Preminger, *An Autobiography* (New York: Doubleday, 1977), p. 202.

14 Ibid.

15 *Film Dope* (UK), No. 3, 1973, p. 2.

16 *Art and Cinema*, Exhibition Catalogue (San Francisco Museum of Art, 1947), p. 13.

17 Of course Otto Preminger was also an émigré, arriving in the United States from Austria in 1936, but unlike Kepes or Moholy-Nagy his European background was in mainstream entertainment and his immediate American destination was Hollywood.

18 *Print* (United States) 15(3), 1961, p. 4.

19 'Absolute film' is a term that generally refers to nonrepresentational films which exploit the medium's formal characteristics and structural properties to produce visual effect.

20 *Bass On Titles* (documentary film), Pyramid Films, USA, 1982.

21 P. Cook (ed.), *The Cinema Book* (London: British Film Institute, 1985), p. 18.

22 S. Guilbaut, *How New York Stole The Idea of Modern Art* (Chicago: University of Chicago Press, 1983), p. 2.

23 For an account of the debate around Guernica see E. Oppler (ed.), *Picasso's Guernica* (New York: Norton, 1988), p. 234.

24 *Graphis* (Switzerland), 9(48), 1953, p. 6.

25 R. Kapsis, *Hitchcock, The Making of a Reputation* (Chicago: University of Chicago Press, 1992), p. 16.

26 The following information is from Kapsis, *Hitchcock*.

27 F. Truffaut, *Hitchcock* (New York: Simon & Schuster, 1984), p. 248.

28 *Vertigo* Press book, 1958.

29 A. Sarris, *Notes on the Auteur Theory* first published in1962, reprinted in G. Mast, M. Cohen and L. Braudy (eds), *Film Theory and Criticism*, 4th edn (Oxford: Oxford University Press, 1992).

30 Museum of Modern Art, New York, Film Library Report, 1956.

31 *Art and Cinema*, San Francisco Museum of Art, p. 19.

32 *Print* (United States) (11)6, 1957, p. 64.

33 W.C. Wees, *Light Moving in Time: Studies in the Visual Aesthetics of Avant Garde Film* (Berkeley: University of California Press, 1992), p. 136.

34 *Films in Review* (United States) 9(6), June/July 1958, p. 333. *The Film Daily* (United States), 14 May 1958, p. 4.

35 Douglas Gordon's *Feature Film* was premiered at the Royal Festival Hall in London on 24 June 2000.

36 Saul Bass, Beverly Hills, 14 July 1992.

7 ✧ Prop goes the easel! Alistair Grant's paintings for *The Rebel*, 1960

Alistair O'Neill

In 1958 the artist Alistair Grant undertook a commission to supply paintings to be used as props for the filming of *The Rebel* (1960), a British comedy film about a repressed city clerk wishing to be taken for an artist, starring Tony Hancock. Grant received the commission after W.A. Whittaker, the producer of the film, visited the Royal College of Art intending to commission the worst student painter to paint some truly awful pictures. In an ambivalently defensive move, designed to either protect the deficiencies of the student or the needs of the working artist, painting tutor Donald Hamilton-Fraser intervened to advise that the young tutor Alistair Grant, recently exhibited at Zwemmer's Gallery, London would be far more suitable.

Grant's commission is an unusual and little-known instance of the Painting School at the Royal College of Art directly serving the commercial needs of industry. As rare offspring of the meeting of high art and mass culture, the paintings received scant attention in their time. They were not considered by the artist to be a 'serious' endeavour and after their use they were thrown away by Elstree Studios as unwanted props. (A portrait of Nanette Newman, who stars as the existentialist Josey in the film, is the surviving exception.) Their lowly status was created by the prevailing view of the time; these were not 'real' paintings as such, but pictures created to the worded requirements of a script, designed to a brief.

When Mrs Knocker of Manchester posed the question 'Does anyone know the whereabouts of Hancock's paintings from his film *The Rebel*?' to the *Notes & Queries* page of the *Guardian* newspaper of 7 October 1991, she began a revival of interest in the condition of a set of paintings long destroyed but still possessed of an affective charge. The folkloric quality granted by the enquiry (one of the paintings later appeared on the cover of a *Notes & Queries* publication) construed them as 'lost' symbols of a bygone era; cheap and popular expressions of their time, transformed by historical distance into commodities so rarefied that their filmic existence places them beyond art market value.

The status of this popular film about a fictional artist has undergone a similar reappraisal. In his study of how the mass cultural products of cinema have represented the high cultural practice of fine art, John A. Walker's *Art & Artists on Screen* is notable for giving balanced analysis across different genres: bio-pics of real artists, films of fictional artists, artists' films and documentaries.[1] The inclusion of *The Rebel* (1960, d. Robert Day) alongside films such as *Spellbound* (1945, d. Alfred Hitchcock), *A Bigger Splash* (1974, d. Jack Hazan) and *Carravaggio* (1985, d. Derek Jarman) establishes a canon that complicates the impact of film on critical and popular understandings of artists and art practice.

Blurring the real and the fictitious, *The Rebel* had an influence both on fine-art practice and on the way that it is read. Lucien Freud is fond of recounting the line from the film 'How do you mix your paints?' 'In a bucket with a big stick.'[2] Also Francis Bacon, who was never one to shy away from secondary source material (his paintings of Van Gogh being directly inspired by watching Vincente Minelli's *Lust for Life*), often talked of paintings looking like they had been ridden over by a bicycle, referring directly to a scene from the film.

In response to Mrs Knocker's question in the *Guardian*, one correspondent wrote: 'There is an exhibition of Picasso's work in Antibes, France, where, in one of the gallery rooms stands Tony Hancock's Aphrodite sculpture. Either that or Picasso was greatly influenced by the School of Hancock.'[3] To claim Picasso as influenced by Hancock is both ridiculous and witty, but the response expresses the tensions between high art and mass culture, fact and fiction, reality and representation, that have established the film and its painted props as ever more memorable.

As designed but economically worthless commodities the paintings are expressive not only of their role within the film, but also of the attitudes that shaped their creation. They were moulded by popular interpretations of art and the practice of art that had been assembled by the scriptwriters Ray Galton and Alan Simpson. The script of *The Rebel* reflects a prevailing unease between the 'realities' of the period and their portrayal, pinpointing the production of the paintings as representative of a transitional moment in popular conceptions of the artist and art practice in post-war Britain.

Reviews of *The Rebel*

Kinematograph Weekly was the main trade magazine for the British cinema industry in the late 1950s. The section 'Reviews for Showman' enabled cinema managers to ascertain which of the forthcoming releases would be worth the financial investment of a booking. Displayed in the table 'New Films at a Glance',[4] *The Rebel* was the only British film advertised for release the week beginning 2 February 1961 against three German, two Mexican, one Swedish and one American. Compared to the wide-screen *Cinemascope* vision of Elvis, the 'exploitable' appeal of *Madeleine 136211* or the veiled attraction of the nature drama *Forbidden Paradise*, Associated British's *The Rebel* seems almost quaint in appeal, relying on traditional British satire for its charm. Conservative in viewpoint, *Kinematograph Weekly*'s criteria for a 'good film' or a box-office success illustrate how the industry equated financial gain with a coherent uninterrupted narrative. The 'tale, sentiment, gags, girls' and ultimately 'happy ending' proved the favoured format. *The Rebel* complies with this recipe; it is not an 'art-house' film, but a mainstream film with the purpose of entertainment. The review explains that notions of art or being artistic are not the predicament of the film, but the setting. Just as Elvis Presley in *Flaming Star* plays a 'half-breed Indian who comes up against acute racial problems' interjected with tuneful songs, so Tony Hancock in *The Rebel* plays a frustrated city clerk who is mistaken for an artistic genius interjected with 'salient cracks'. Yet the review states an added dimension: 'Although the humour is mostly visual, audiences may not fully appreciate it unless they have some knowledge of the subject guyed.'[5]

The Rebel operates both as a form of entertainment with a star, setting and story-line, and a satirical study requiring additional knowledge for full comprehension. *Kinematograph Weekly* predicted that the film 'should attract both the beret and the cap and muffler trade'.[6] According to the article 'Ancock Triumphant and They Were All There'[7] published later that month in the same title, the prediction was realised. In addition to the usual guests at the film's première, there were also a number of leading artists, Royal Academicians and students from London's various art schools. The two Royal Academicians present at the première, Carel Weight and Ruskin Spear, were also teachers in the RCA Painting School.

For the première, the long entrance foyer of the Plaza was 'set out as an art gallery exhibiting paintings from the film'.[8] This was not Grant's idea nor his exhibition, but a publicity stunt by the marketing department of Associated British which maintained the fiction of Hancock as *auteur* into the première. In the eyes of the cinema industry, the contribution of Grant and the RCA to the making of *The Rebel* was negligible. The only credit Grant received was a cursory mention in the title sequence. The attitude toward the contribution was not solely the opinion of the cinema industry, but one also prevalent in the Painting School itself.

The Painting School in the 1950s

When Derek Boshier arrived at the Royal College of Art in the Autumn of 1959, the dress and demeanour of the students of the Painting School were in keeping with the parts they had recently played as extras in the filming of the Joyce Cary novel *The Horse's Mouth*, shot a year earlier. The film concerned the life of Gulley Jimson (played by Alec Guinness), an old, impoverished painter loosely based on the Soho socialite Geralde Wilde. The main painting used in this film was *Adam and Eve*, painted by John Bratby, a star student and now tutor of the Painting School. (The painting reappeared at the RCA for the British Art Fair 2000. Although it gained much press coverage, the painting remained unsold.) This painting had a 'kitchen sink' appeal that was reflective of the student intake of the RCA in the late 1950s.

Due to the interruption of war or national service, many older men were entering postgraduate education. Also, ex-servicemen's families were receiving grants that enabled younger men and women, previously disadvantaged by background, to gain a postgraduate education in the arts. The RCA pursued an admissions policy that openly embraced risk. The artist Malcolm Morley (student 1954–57) serves as a particularly good example of this approach. A working-class student, Morley was accepted on the course by the Rector of the College, Robin Darwin, on the merit of the paintings he created while serving time in prison for robbery. Reflecting on the student body, Darwin wrote in the Annual Report of 1959 that

> The student of today is less easy to teach because the chips on his shoulder, which in some instances are virtual professional epaulettes, make him less ready to learn; yet this refusal to take ideas on trust, though it may not be congenial to the tutor, may in the long run prove to be a valuable characteristic. The students of today are much more extraordinarily dressed and a lot dirtier and this no doubt reflects the philosophy of the 'beat' generation.[9]

The observation on the dress and philosophy of the students was symptomatic of an awareness of the student body as distinct not only from the staff at the RCA, but also from students at other educational institutions. This also came to the attention of the national press. The *Evening Standard* newspaper reported on a party thrown by the College in 1955:

> Five hundred tramps converged in South Kensington to attend the worst-dressed party of the year. They came in converted dust lorries and broken down ex-taxis. The men wore tattered suits and dented top-hats. The girls were in moth-eaten blouses, straw hats and woollen bedroom slippers ... Later many students settled on the dance floor to sleep until dawn, lulled by the guitar music from Professor John Skeaping, Head of the Sculpture School.[10]

The notoriety of the College as a whole was driven by Robin Darwin who expected his staff, who he believed to be at the forefront of their respective fields, to continue their practice while teaching. The Royal College received expansive coverage both in the arts and in the lifestyle sections of British newspapers and magazines. An article in a 1958 edition of *Tatler* proclaimed Carel Weight to be the ideal society portrait painter, while a 1960 *Homes and Gardens* piece titled 'Arbiters of Taste' illustrated the interior decoration of the studios of the Painting staff.

The courting of the newly emerging media was also evident in the student magazine *Ark*. In the late 1950s this magazine took on a highly professional profile, establishing itself at the vanguard of emerging print technologies and graphic design, and gaining multi-national advertisers and an international impact. In issue number 27 of *Ark*, the student editor Ken Baynes featured a transcript of a sketch called 'Economy Drive' taken from *Hancock's Half Hour*. This was the only recorded instance of collaboration between the institution and the scriptwriters bar Grant's commission. Asked about the depiction of the tortured artist in *The Rebel*, Baynes draws clear connection between the activities of the Painting School and the popular depiction of creative practitioners:

> I think it's an idea that applied very strongly to those who immediately preceded our time; you know, the Dylan Thomas image of artists behaving badly, tremendously put in Joyce Cary's book 'The Horse's Mouth'. Gulley Jimson is the archetypal artist of that period and although I can't imagine that masses of people read the book, that image of the artist was a very accessible and accepted one. And of course John Bratby actually painted the pictures for the film and the students designed the cover for the book.[11]

Bratby later complained that his work had become too heavily associated with a fictitious account of a stubborn, cantankerous artist. The enmeshing of literary and filmic depictions of artists with actual accounts of the activities of the staff and students at the Painting School not only aided popular definitions of art practice, but also acted as source material for the scriptwriters of *The Rebel*. Ideas about the status of popular culture were actively contested within the pages of *Ark* magazine; the transcript of *Hancock's Half Hour* was part of an actively pluralistic definition of culture. The script of *The Rebel* tried to achieve something similar.

The script

The script for *The Rebel*, in particular a second revised version dated 23 May 1960, reveals the level of detail that the scriptwriters gave to Grant to devise the *Infantile* paintings. It also shows that certain situations or scenes from the film were crafted around contentious artworks of the day. The following passage describes Hancock's studio in the room he rents from Mrs Cravate:

INTERIOR. TONY'S STUDIO. DAY.

Tony's eyeline: it is a huge half-finished statue of an Epstein like figure of a nude. It is a horrible monstrosity. Tony's face takes on an exultant expression of sheer joy and wonder as he admires his creation ...
... We now RUN ROUND the room and see the other works. Done by him. There are loads of very amateurish paintings. The sort of thing a child does. The sun with the lines coming out of it for the rays, the sea represented by a wavy line etc., and a few modernist Picasso like paintings. There are assorted sculptures, ranging from reclining figures to modern things with holes all over them, and 'unknown political prisoners' made from wire. All the work of an untutored mediocrity.[12]

In this scripted description, Galton and Simpson reveal that their definition of Hancock's style is an amalgam of artists and artworks recognised through their derision by the British popular press. Thus, Jacob Epstein merits attention for 'The Cult of Ugliness' he spread through the fabric of London with his public sculptures.[13] The 'unknown political prisoners' are a direct reference to the international sculpture competition to design a monument to the Unknown Political Prisoner won by Reg Butler, whose model was destroyed by a Hungarian refugee while it was on display in the Tate Gallery in 1953.[14]

In the face of these kinds of reaction, the Arts Council of Great Britain had made efforts to popularise modern sculpture. Galton and Simpson were probably aware of this campaign, and the following passage taken from the catalogue for the 1958 travelling exhibition *Sculpture for the Home* should be considered against the scene from *The Rebel* which showed Hancock in the process of creating a huge sculpture in a rented room:

In 1946, when the first exhibition of this series was shown in several provincial galleries, it was by no means common for collectors to acquire sculpture for their homes in the same way as they bought paintings or drawings. The growing reputation of British sculpture, the open air exhibitions in Battersea and Holland Parks, and not least these small travelling exhibitions have changed people's views considerably and accustomed them to the idea of living with sculpture.

Although bronzes may still be relatively expensive, the new materials used by sculptors today have brought their work within the range of the least affluent collector.[15]

To return to Grant's brief (he had nothing to do with any of the sculptures, most were made by the prop department at Elstree Studios), it is clear that Galton and Simpson were looking for work that appeared to be that of an amateur painter. The Annual Report of the Arts Council for 1959–60 emphasises the role of amateur activities in maintaining and spreading cultural activity within the period:

> They can certainly foster an interest in the arts and within their accepted limits they are a powerful auxiliary of diffusion. In many parts of the land they will continue, except, for the wireless, to provide the only possible form of irrigation.[16]

While amateur artists were seen as important for their role in promoting an interest in the arts, scant attention was paid to the quality of their output. They found themselves marginalised, recognised only as proof that the Arts Council's message was getting across. Television was treated in a similar manner in the same report:

> Despite it's weekend habit of accepting the lowest common denominator of taste, it already has to its credit many bold and imaginative experiments in bringing the fine arts home to millions who have enjoyed no more than a marginal acquaintance with them.[17]

This is a theme to which I would like return to in discussion of the arts programme *Monitor*. For the moment it is interesting to note that Galton and Simpson, trained in radio and television, picked the character of the amateur artist to raise questions about the tensions between high and low culture.

The Infantiles and the primitive

Grant's brief was to supply three sets of paintings, representing three different artistic intentions (hence three different styles) each distinguishable from the other. The first were those supposedly painted by Hancock in the style of 'The Infantile' (a fictional grandiose art term for the style of someone who cannot paint with technique, but whose work bears a resemblance to primitive art); the second, the work of the artist in the film, Paul Ashbee (fairly naturalistic figuration); and lastly the work of Ashbee under the influence of Hancock's 'Infantiles'. The paintings that Grant had exhibited at Zwemmer's were used as Ashbee's unadulterated work.

The mixture of the amateur and primitive was intended to raise the problems encountered in distinguishing between 'high' and 'low' cultural forms. The conferring of artistic legitimacy on primitive works often leads people to feel uncomfortable and misled. Several British television programmes have explored this issue, for instance Desmond Morris's exhibition of paintings by Congo the chimpanzee.[18]

The combination of the amateur and the primitive displayed in the Infantile painting *Ducks in Flight*, as shown early in the film, demonstrates how the icons of domestic art were used as subject matter. Grant recalled 'flying ducks are a naff idea in a sitting room aren't they?'[19] Grant may have ridiculed the subject matter, but the image itself is arresting. It sits somewhat uncomfortably between an amateur, a primitive and an informed picture. It is likely that Grant found the stylistic expression to make such a picture during his time at the Royal College of Art.

Under the title 'Buckett of Battersea', an article published in 1953 in *Picture Post* claimed the discovery of a British 'primitive'. The painter concerned, Mr Fred Buckett, was a general labourer at the Victoria and Albert Museum and was often sent to clean up after the painting students in an annex of temporary studios attached to the museum. Surrounded by student endeavour Buckett decided 'that student work – I never could take to it. I thought I might improve on it'.[20] The popularity of his efforts, hung in a makeshift gallery that doubled as the washroom, gained him the admiration of the students. His stance precisely matches Hancock's in *The Rebel*, an older unskilled worker who aims to enter into a younger artistic scene and is then accepted. His naiveté is tinged with humour: 'The original "Grass on Whitewash" was covered with a hunting scene. – My wife argued the point, saying she'd never seen trees out of leaf during the hunting season – and she was right – so I said they're out of practice.'[21]

As in *The Rebel*, an art critic was called in to validate the work of the 'primitive'. In the *Picture Post* piece, John Russell, critic for the *Sunday*

7.1 Ronald Searle 'The Rake's Progress: The Painter' published in *Punch*, 1954.

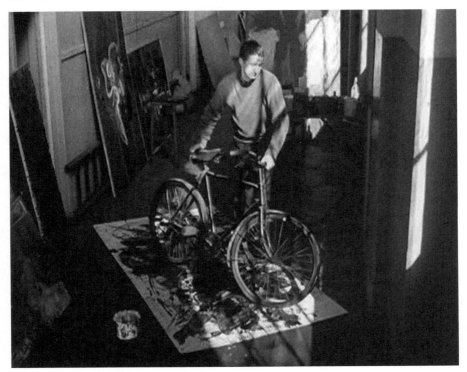

7.2 William Green at the Royal College of Art, 1958.

Times offered qualified praise for Buckett's work: 'He has a natural (not a naturalistic) colour sense; and with this (witness "Bob the Cat") a feeling for the monumental that many an Academician might envy.'[22] Buckett's paintings bear close similarities to Grant's paintings in their palette of colour, composition, scale of subject to frame and flatness in application.

This was not the only direct reference in *The Rebel* to painting activity at the RCA. The action paintings of William Green, some of which were produced by riding a bicycle over a canvas, had been featured in an article in *Life* magazine and in a short film by Ken Russell screened on BBC's *Tonight* programme, both from 1958.[23] The dissemination of unorthodox approaches to fine-art practice through the medium of popular television had a marked effect. 'Green instantly

7.3 Film still: 'Bicycle on Canvas', from *The Rebel*, 1960.

became notorious, seeming to epitomise everything that the general public expected of an avant-garde artist.'[24] Later Green's methods were appropriated for comic ends by the scriptwriters for *The Rebel*, who had Hancock making additional use of a cow's hooves for one desired pictorial effect.

Other reference points for the film include *The Rake's Progress: The Painter*,[25] a cartoon by Ronald Searle that formed part of a series published in *Punch* magazine in the mid-1950s. Based on the series of the same title (1694–1767) by William Hogarth, they depict the downfall of a man of easy virtue. Searle transposed this to the life of a painting student at the RCA. Searle's artist rake entered the art world through an institutional route, partook in its absurdities and ended up a figure of the establishment, interested in status rather than creativity.

In this cartoon Searle was arguing that in 1955, a painter's future career lay in a string of acquaintances of his teachers and Darwin. Darwin himself is shown creating links between society and the protégés of the RCA, and Searle was suggesting that the artist had little control of this process. The disparity between this career path and those of the Pop generation of only five years later is revealed in David Hockney's interpretation of *The Rake's Progress* (1961–3). Set in New York, it concerns Hockney's struggle for individual identity in the aspirational artistic capital, the opposite of Searle's legitimised British path. There are situations in *The Rebel* that mirror the six tableaux of Searle's series. Thus the article on Fred Buckett, Russell's film about William Green and the Searle cartoon, all reportage on the Painting School at the RCA, were fundamental to the script and the paintings produced for *The Rebel* (see Figures 7.1, 7.2, 7.3).

To an extent Galton and Simpson's approach was not consciously ironic but merely uninformed. In the words of John Russell on the subject of the British 'primitive', 'Mr Buckett sticks to what he knows well and cuts the rest out of the newspapers'.[26] In my interview with them, the scriptwriter Simpson and the painter Grant described a similar process, as this extract reveals:

> *Alistair O'Neill:* What kinds of source material did you draw upon when you were writing the script for the film?
>
> *Alan Simpson:* I think we might have got some jargon out of books, some art books. But certainly when Hancock was talking it was all rubbish because the whole point was he didn't know what he was talking about and we didn't know what we were all talking about so we just sort of made it up and made it sound pretentious. In fact we had to have George Sanders making sense because he was an art critic and we had to have the other painters making sense. So I think if there was any art jargon in there we probably got it from art magazines.
>
> *Alistair Grant:* Sunday papers.
>
> *Ian Simpson:* I always remember George [Sanders], he used to put a couple of lines in himself. We had a line when he was admiring one of the Paul Massey paintings and his line went 'Oh, such beautiful tones', and George suddenly came out with 'Such chiaroscuro'.

Alistair Grant: Oh no, he came out with 'Camera obscura' because I said to you, 'That's not right, it should be chiaroscuro'. So Ray [Galton] said 'You're the bloody art expert, so you can go and tell him'. So I went up and I said 'It's not camera obscura it's chiaroscuro' and he said, 'I was using the northern Italian pronunciation.'[27]

As an approach, this process is similar to the cut-and-paste techniques used in early British Pop art, for example Eduardo Paolozzi's scrapbooks. An even more important similarity is the film's use of humour, an essential part of the pleasure of Pop. The film fits within Pop's attempt to question, bridge the gap or erode 'on the one hand the serious, the artistic and the political and on the other the ephemeral, the commercial and the pleasurable'.[28] To understand the full meaning of the film as part of popular culture, it is essential to understand the character played by the comedian Tony Hancock in the programme *Hancock's Half Hour*: Anthony Aloysius St John Hancock.

Hancock and the Uninformed

Starting in 1944 as a radio series, *Hancock's Half Hour* was conceived as 'non-domestic with no jokes and no funny voices, just relying on caricature and situation humour'.[29] The maturing of this comedy during its transition from radio to television and ultimately to film bore fruit in *The Rebel*'s central character, a frustrated city clerk with artistic aspirations. Galton and Simpson's preoccupation with establishing a 'reality' led to the location of 23 Railway Cuttings, East Cheam as the situation for most episodes. This reality, a naturalism of language, characterisation and location allowing for almost-believable story lines and audience identification led to a comedy of observation in a world the audience recognised. In contrast to the vaudevillian and variety show-style slapstick of the 1940s, *Hancock's Half Hour* was a comedy of the mundane which possessed an underlying critique of the supposed affluence of the 1950s.

Expressed through the character of Hancock, 'the seedy misfit with intellectual pretensions, [was] sure he was missing out while those around him never had it so good'.[30] It was suggestive of segregative opportunity, representing an aesthetic of boredom rather than an aesthetic of plenty. In 'The Missing Page', for instance, Hancock, much to the delight of the librarian, asks for copies of works by Homer, Plato, Bestead and Ulbricht only to earn the librarian's contempt when he uses them as a stand to reach the top shelf of the crime section for a copy of *Lady Don't Fall Backwards*.

> *Tony Hancock*: I read thrillers purely as relaxation between the heavy stuff. I find fifty pages of *Dead Dames Don't Talk* the perfect hors-d'oeuvre to an all night bash at Bertrand Russell's.
>
> *Sid James*: Bertrand Russell, didn't he write *Kiss the Blood Off My Hands*?
>
> *Tony Hancock*: *Kiss the Blood Off My Hands*? Bertie of all people, of course he didn't. That's not his style at all. You're thinking of Aldous Huxley.[31]

Setting himself up as a student of culture, Hancock's position is aspirational and linked to improvement. His location on the suburban periphery marks his interaction with a culture aimed at the mass rather than the minority. It is apparent that Hancock's wish is not to gain mere knowledge, but to move along the social strata. The humour in these situations often lies in his confusion between forms of culture, a confusion which reveals his social standing.

Hancock-esque confusion was found beyond the domain of comedy. The pioneering arts programme *Monitor* (1958–1965) was an open-ended series loosely held together by its presenter and editor Huw Wheldon. The show maintained a progressive attitude and a broad definition of culture, and took a liberal, open-minded view. Like *The Rebel* it did not assume the viewer required specialist knowledge to watch the programme, yet it also catered for a specialist audience. In spite of this, Weldon was very ignorant of the contemporary visual arts: he thought *collage* was a person, had never heard of Marcel Duchamp before a programme was made on the artist, and famously failed to recognise the actress Brigitte Bardot in a film.[32] Galton and Simpson were not alone in their unrefined view of contemporary art practice.

Monitor was responsible for commissioning the 1962 Ken Russell film *Pop Goes the Easel* which featured students and staff from the Painting School. Depicting the lives of Peter Blake, Derek Boshier, Pauline Boty and Peter Phillips, it concentrated on their romantic consumption of popular culture rather than the artistic process, or any form of critical evaluation. Russell wanted the film to echo the pace of the subject matter and employed experimental cutting and use of sound. On seeing the rough version, Wheldon insisted that Russell should include shots of the artists painting in order to ensure that they would be considered as serious painters. 'In what was surely a sardonic gesture, Russell employed some classical music for the soundtrack at this point.'[33] Derek Boshier remembers the outrage the programme caused, not solely in subject matter, but also because of the painters' working-class accents, 'at a time when people read the news on the radio in their dinner jackets'.[34]

The tension between a dinner jacket and a working-class accent, the expectation of what an artist does and how it should be documented, marks a transitional moment. Hancock explored this moment in *The Rebel*, his character changing from frustrated artist to accepted society portrait painter back to Sunday painter. Hancock's ability to move across social characters and distinctions is rebellious; however, this is not a notion of rebellion drawn from the masculine American model. Rather, the Hancock character's self-assurance and the need to burn ever brighter are coupled to a very British sense of self-doubt and withdrawal. This is essential to Hancock's comic success:

> Perhaps one reason for the success of Hancock shows is that they stay close to life as known by their audiences, finding humour in popular newspapers and double-feature film programmes or putting Hancock in the sort of situation where we all feel ineffectual.[35]

The merit of *The Rebel* emerges from its expression of the anxiety felt by many in distinguishing between authentic and inauthentic strands of contemporary art – not only in practice, but also in documentation and dissemination. Even though *The Rebel* fails to identify New York as the artistic capital in 1960 and instead relies on the antiquated but recognisable 'Sacre Coeur out the window' representation of Paris, it pinpoints the view of British society in the late 1950s toward 'the art world'.[36] (Notably, the film bombed in New York in October 1961 where it was screened with the title *Call Me Genius*). In a period where the values of affluence and prosperity for the masses were measured by the consumption of cultural commodities often alien to them, *The Rebel* encapsulates British society's apprehensive view of the 'bad new times' articulated through the expression of 'the good old ones'.

As an enjoyable form of popular culture, films like *The Rebel* have often been regarded as 'too ephemeral or light to be worthy of sustained enquiry'.[37] It is easy to treat fictional or non-fictional representations of artistic activity as misleading in their pursuit of the authentic through the inauthentic, as contrary to the hard-won values of high art. Yet these representations and their role in forming society's opinions toward an understanding of art and art practice should not be underestimated. A survey of 1992 asked a cross-section of British society to name a well-known artist.[38] With 38 per cent more votes than Rembrandt, Van Gogh or Constable was TV personality Rolf Harris, who first made his name presenting popular arts programmes featuring his distinctive style of caricature drawing. In December 2001 Harris presented an arts programme for BBC1 on the Impressionists. It seems that the unsophisticated or irreverent position on art practice may have won the upper hand.

Postscript

Since this material was written, The Department of Reconstructive Archaeology at The London Institute of 'Pataphysics, published 'Encomia for Anthony Hancock' edited by Alastair Brotchie and Magnus Irvin in 2002. The catalogue accompanied an exhibition at the Foundry Gallery, London (8–20 September 2002) that recreated and displayed all of the artworks featured in *The Rebel*. At the back of the catalogue is an obituary for Alistair Grant (1925–1997) written by Galton and Simpson. It ends:

> Alistair Grant will be forever remembered for his influence on the Infantalists. To this day, many art critics and connoisseurs insist that a great proportion of the works hitherto attributed to Hancock and his acolyte Paul Ashby were in fact painted by Grant. This is open to question but could be explained by the appearance of a 'paintings by' credit given to him in the 1960 bio-pic *The Rebel*, a flawed, badly written, low-budget, trashy, highly romanticised and poorly researched hagiography of the life and work of Hancock. Grant surely deserves better than this.

Notes

1 J.A. Walker, *Art and Artists on Screen* (Manchester: Manchester University Press, 1993).

2 D. Farson, 'Beneath the Skin', *Guardian*, 6 September 1993, p. 2.

3 *Guardian*, 14 October 1991, p. 23.

4 *Kinematograph Weekly*, 2 February 1961, p. 18.

5 Ibid.

6 Ibid.

7 *Kinematograph Weekly*, 23 February 1961.

8 Ibid.

9 *Royal College of Art Annual Report* (London, 1959), p. 20.

10 *Evening Standard*, 26 February 1955, p. 36.

11 Interview with Ken Baynes, conducted by Jean MacIntyre, 13 February 1995.

12 *The Rebel*, film script, second revised version, 23 May 1960 (London: British Film Institute Library), unpaginated.

13 The 'Cult of Ugliness' was the title of a letter sent to the *Manchester Guardian* by Sir Reginald Blomfield, Past President of the Institute of British Architects on the Epstein sculptures commissioned for the London Underground Headquarters at St James's Park, London, 1929. In J. Epstein, *Epstein: An Autobiography* (London: Vista Books, 1955), p. 270.

14 P. Heron, *The Changing Forms of Art* (London: Routledge & Kegan Paul, 1955), pp. 43–4.

15 *Sculpture for the Home*, exhibition catalogue, Arts Council, 1958, unpaginated.

16 'Amateur Influence', *Arts Council Annual Report* 1959–60, unpaginated.

17 'The Impact of Television', *Arts Council Annual Report* 1959–60, unpaginated.

18 D. Morris, *The Biology of Art: A Study of the Picture-making Behaviour of the Great Apes and its Relationship to Human Art* (London: Methuen, 1962).

19 Interview with Alistair Grant, Ray Galton and Alan Simpson conducted by the author, February 1995.

20 *Picture Post*, 14 November 1953, p. 28.

21 Ibid.

22 Ibid.

23 *Life International*, 'A Boom in US Art Abroad', 7 July 1958, p. 68. 'Making an Action Painting', 1957, short silent film by Ken Russell, *Tonight*, BBC Television.

24 W. Green, *The Susan Hayward Exhibition* (London: England & Co., 1993).

25 First published in *Punch*, 1955. Reprinted in the *Tribune*, 5 March 1955.

26 *Picture Post*, 14 November 1953, p. 49.

27 Interview with Grant, Galton and Simpson, February 1995.

28 D. Hebdige, *Hiding in the Light: On Images and Things* (London: Comedia, 1988), p. 126.

29 J. Corner (ed.), *Popular Television in Britain* (London: British Film Institute Publishing, 1991), p. 78.

30 Ibid.

31 *The Missing Page*, BBC TV, transmitted 26 February1960.

32 J.A. Walker, *Arts TV* (London: John Libbey & Co.), 1993, p. 46.

33 Ibid., p. 33.

34 Interview with Derek Boshier, conducted by the author, February 1995.

35 R. Galton and A. Simpson, *Hancock's Half Hour* (London: Woburn Press, 1974), p. 132.

36 Interview with Grant, Galton and Simpson, February 1995.

37 Walker, *Art and Artists*, p. 111.

38 Survey results at www.theage.com/entertainment accessed 9 April 2001.

8 ✧ Design in the monochrome box: the BBC Television design department and the modern style, 1946–1962

Michelle Jones

In the intimate history of most British families in the Fifties, the day the television came forms a sort of post-war watershed. For many thousands the very act of acquisition, a financial transaction, practically obligatory yet larger than had ever before been undertaken, acted as a kind of initiation into the new consumers' society.[1]

WITHIN BROADCASTING HISTORY, the 1950s was to be a defining decade for television. Public insatiability for the medium began to establish television viewing as a central activity of the British home. Its pervasive nature can be said not only to have restructured the domestic patterns and social habits of individual households, but also to have played an influential role within the nation's consumer culture. Television brought the public sphere into the private home, endowing it with the potential to manipulate the predilection of the individual consumer. Its visual nature presented a further tool of mass communication that in terms of design sensibility offered a unique potential to influence public taste.

The post-war years were a time of national, economic, social and cultural transition, through which public taste was persistently targeted by the agencies of design reform and the design profession. This attention aimed to encourage an appreciation and consumption of one dominant, culturally legitimate aesthetic, embodied within the stylistic authority – contemporary design. This neo-modernist style demonstrated its commitment to both the governing values of 'good design' and consumer preference through its humanising use of new materials, forms and techniques. The post-war years were to fuel a growing idealism that this form of design was something important and beneficial to the everyday lives of ordinary men and women. This commitment and belief corresponded with the egalitarian mood of both the country and the BBC (British Broadcasting Corporation)'s public-service philosophy. Television was to be harnessed to promote the rhetoric and dictates of post-war design reform, initially through programmes devoted to the subject and subsequently through the activity of the BBC's newly formed Design Department that furnished and controlled every visual element contained within the screen.

Focusing on specific television settings created during the 1950s, this study offers an analysis of the reasons behind the ubiquitous permeation of contemporary style into all aspects of BBC television design. In 1962 Richard Levin, Head of the Design Department, proclaimed that television 'at one designer to a million audience' had produced 'a new breed of "tastemakers" whose eventual effect on style and fashion would be hard to assess'.[2] His statement forms the basis of this enquiry which, through an assessment of television's role within the propagation and acceptance of 'good design', examines the extent to which the BBC's designers operated as taste-makers to the nation.

Television: a design forum for national improvement

The BBC saw itself as administering a service in the national interest; the underlining spirit that informed all of its work stemmed from the legacy of John Reith, its first Director General. His ideology, generically termed 'Reithianism', dictated that the Corporation use the 'brute force' of its monopoly to give the public 'everything that was best in every department of human knowledge, endeavour and achievement', to give them what they ought to want since 'few knew what they wanted and fewer what they needed'.[3] This innate paternalism ensured that from the outset, television was to instigate a policy of design promotion that was coherent with the BBC's ambitions to use the medium, like radio before it, as an instrument of national improvement.

As early as 1945 the BBC had joined forces with the newly created Council of Industrial Design, the principle voice of the British government's post-war campaign for 'good design', in order to influence the taste of the viewing public and establish a wider acceptance of modern design. Internal BBC memos show that the official justification for cooperation with the Council were not aesthetic but economic; 'to reach manufacturers and the British housewife'. They wanted, first, to encourage those manufacturers who, left to their own devices, would not produce competitively designed goods and, secondly, to raise public awareness, particularly among post-war women, 'who having worked with machinery would now have a new idea of what they should have in household equipment.'[4] The Second World War had taken its toll on Britain's manufacturing industries, and consequently what was needed to stimulate and revive the country's trade links were products designed to appeal to the international market. The acceptance by British manufacturers and retailers of this forward-looking design paradigm was seen as an essential element within the nation's post-war economic reconstruction.

To convince manufacturers of the existence of a market both at home and abroad for this internationally auspicious style, it was first necessary to convert British consumer taste and demand. In accordance with this, both television and radio didactically featured design within programme debates. However, with the realisation that manufacturers' customs and consumer preference could not be modified through promotional rhetoric alone, visual presentation was suggested as a more beneficial way to accustom the public to the new style. The Council of Industrial Design and the BBC subsequently explored the prospect of incorporating products of modern design into the furnishing and backgrounds of television programmes.

It was throughout this period that the system of television was being developed and classified, when the BBC was specifying what it was, how it should circulate and, most importantly for a visual medium, how it should look. By 1952, with this evolution taking place, the relationship between the BBC and the Council floundered, as it was felt the Council was not enabling television 'to keep abreast of the times'.[5] Though both organisations were committed to mutual aims, bureaucratic and financial squabbles ultimately thwarted their alliance. Before the 1950s, the visual aspects of television illustrated a lack of invention and experiment. As the decade progressed, it became apparent that the Council's authoritative advice on debates and set dressing and its system of lending furniture was inadequate. Creative personnel were required to formulate and guide television's visual appearance. The task required television practitioners with vision and knowledge of the changing world of modern design trends, employed within an in-house department, devoted specifically to the Corporation's design. This realisation led to the appointment of Richard Levin, in 1953, to head and develop a formal Design Department.

With a staff of 110, Levin controlled all the scenic resources of the BBC both solid and pictorial. From his first day he proved to be a proselytiser, regarding television as a visual medium, an obvious but insufficiently recognised point. He believed that the consistent use of good modern design within television settings would have significance beyond the practical and aesthetic enrichment of programme presentation. As he was to state, 'The Public have little or no response to pictorial beauty or ugliness ... television is an opportunity to develop visual sensibility in the audience that is already willing to use their eyes for hours on end in the daily pursuit of entertainment.'[6] Even *The Times* newspaper's announcement of his appointment commented that he was 'particularly conscious of the effect on taste, which the choice of television properties may have'.[7]

Prior to this appointment, Levin was an established freelance designer, with his own practice, specialising in exhibition work. He had previous connections with the BBC through designing its public exhibitions for two decades. During these years, he had developed a bold yet simple style to project a dignified public image for the Corporation. This style relied on graphics and photography and was derivative of the austere discipline of exhibition design first sponsored in Britain in the 1930s by companies such as ICI and Shell who commissioned continental designers. It is discernible in Levin's later design work that throughout the inter-war period he had worked on exhibitions with Maholy Nagy and other European émigrés designers who introduced him to the language of International Modernism.[8] The Ministry of Information's Exhibition Division, an important training ground for young designers in graphic and display techniques, had also employed him during the Second World War. These influences were to assist in Levin's formulation of and belief in 'good design'. This understanding was also translated into a specific ideal of 'good taste', an aesthetic judgement that corresponded with that of the cultural elite of

British design reform. More often than not the protagonists of this circle operated through a 'shared taste' that was embodied within contemporary design's aesthetic language rather than the rational dictates of the Modern Movement they claimed to champion. It was Levin and his appointed teams' personal commitment to this shared taste, which they believed came from training and discrimination and was not a simple result of the improvement of industrial design, that ensured the style's rising to prominence within television's designs in the second half of the 1950s.

By appointing a Head of Department from the field of exhibition design rather than the world of film or theatre, it was obvious from 1953 onward that the practice of television design was to follow a new visual course. The BBC's Design Department, under this guidance, was led into a crusade to formulate a visual policy for an industry largely indifferent to the role of design in its visual output. Since 1946 when television transmission had resumed, post-war restrictions and the limited availability of production materials had severely impeded the Department's activity. The BBC's senior management's principal concern had been that the continual flow of programme output did not take place against the bare studio walls.[9] Initially they employed twelve designers, all with film or theatre backgrounds, who transposed the language of these disciplines into the medium of television, so that it developed an orientation, as far as scenery was concerned, toward the needs of dramatic productions. Levin was to subsequently announce in disgust that the rest of its visual output, particularly within the areas of 'Light Entertainment' and 'Talks', was inherited from 'the worst of Music Hall, Pantomime, Pier End, Concert Party, Cabaret and Hollywood Musical traditions'.[10]

Although television's initial presentation, outlook and style was developed from these popular traditions and accustomed forms of communication, it was immediately apparent to Levin that, despite these similarities, its production requirements were entirely unique. These older mediums may have given television design its foundation and initial practitioners, but in fact, television's origins lay in radio broadcasting and verbal communication rather than visual entertainment. Consequently the aesthetics of television developed from a hybrid of exhibition, graphic and advertising techniques, which corresponded with the BBC's predominant public-service philosophy and prioritised information and education over artistry.

The studio design unit and the development of the BBC 'house-style'

A significant arena for television design was offered by the studio-based programmes emanating from the BBC Talks department. The design for these on-screen interviews and debates needed to impart information and create a general educational atmosphere. The notion that design was as crucial to talks programmes as it was to drama became Levin's first priority. He began to guide his inherited designers to create what were seen as more 'intelligent' and 'tasteful' environments and to rid the genre of its previously established tradition of 'phoney room sets' with their 'obligatory view through a window' and their particular inclination to represent the BBC's studio as a type of gentleman's club.[11] The intention was to replace these former conventions with modern, sophisticated and neutral backgrounds that used space, shape, light and shadows to define the televised area. Since this type of informative programme was seen by a large cross-section of the general audience it was hoped that, through the imaginative use of artistic set pieces, modern materials and well-designed furnishings, it would influence popular taste.

Asian Club in 1953 was the first programme where Levin put these theories into practice (see Figure 8.1) and he has described the setting for this show as 'television's first truly designed scenery for Talks'.[12] The set requirements for the series were chairs for the participants to sit on and drapes to separate the scene from the studio. This offered Levin a perfect opportunity to demonstrate that well-designed furniture and fabrics with adequate lighting could enrich the visual texture on the screen. He chose to incorporate 'good design' through his use of Ernest Race's BA3 chairs, while introducing aspects of exhibition design into the background, through the inclusion of transparent flats to create interesting light sources, interspersed with painted panels that gave it depth and dimension.

The next programme of significance to receive similar attention was a popular celebrity chat show entitled *Joan Gilbert's Diary*. The Council

8.1 The set of the television programme *Asian Club*, 1953.

of Industrial Design, in a continuation of its previous role, supplied the furniture to create a permanent background penthouse set (see Figure 8.2). Levin personally dressed this particular programme as a demonstration of his ideals, so that his employees would 'know what he was talking about' and would incorporate similarly tasteful aspects into their own design work.[13]

Despite these initial inroads, the impact of the evolving Design Department on the output of television was not immediately visible. Its infrastructure was in a state of disarray and the flow of television's output was chaotic, leaving little time for thought, creativity and realisation. In 1956, three years after Levin's appointment, Bernard Hollowood, who had been involved in many of the BBC's and Council's promotional initiatives of the 1940s, offered a disappointing consideration of the aesthetic content of television:

> There was a time when I regarded television as a potentially powerful instrument of propaganda for good taste and good design. It seemed to me that this new window on the world would lead us gradually,

8.2 The set of the television programme *Joan Gilbert's Diary*, 1953.

by example rather than by ratiocination towards an appreciation of formal and patterned excellence in such things as furniture, fabrics, pottery, lettering, and decor. If people looked in nightly upon a studio scene vetted for taste by experts in industrial design it was unlikely, I argued, that they could avoid its improving influence. We should become a nation of Bauhaus disciples, of Herbert Read's and Gordon Russell's. Well I was wildly out of my reckoning. Television, I regret to say does very little for industrial design, no more than the cinema and the theatre.[14]

The Design Department's new directives were obviously having little discernible impact on the Corporation's visual output. Internal correspondence from March 1955 illustrated that Levin had already realised that in order to raise the profile and standard of the BBC Design Department, he needed to bring in an outside group of industrial designers. He turned to his former colleagues from the Ministry of Information's Exhibition Division whose Design Research Unit he thought of as the leading design group in the country, and recommended that the BBC place them under contract. In a written communication to the Controller of Programming he demanded the establishment of 'a television group under the direction of Misha Black and Milner Gray' (the Unit's founders) on an exclusive basis, to carry out twenty-four annual productions. This union could then provide 'not only a cushion for increased output', but also an 'incentive' to television's established designers, that would 'inevitably lead to an improvement in design, by example'.[15] This partnership led to only one production, a 'Spanish Ballet' designed by Misha Black, and the permanent appointment by the BBC of Clifford Hatts from the Unit.[16] Unfortunately it did not develop any further – due to time constraints, the heavy commitment of the Consultancy to outside projects and the pace of television's production which allowed little time for preliminary instructions in the technicalities of television work. Such freelance industrial designers ultimately failed to offer the answer to television's design problems.

Fortunately this dilemma was resolved by the steady expansion of television ownership from the middle of the decade onward which increased the Department's budget and facilitated the recruitment of a new type of designer trained in architecture, display and interior and exhibition design. One of the earliest of these appointments was Natasha Kroll who had led the window-display team at the department store Simpsons of Piccadilly in London from 1942 until 1955, when she was head-hunted for the BBC. Like many who subsequently entered the profession, she had met Levin while working on the Festival of Britain, where she collaborated on the displays in his Land Travelling Exhibition.[17] Her work for Simpsons had garnered attention and respect from design circles, where her attitude to presentation was considered to be 'enlightened and unconventional'.[18] Having already established a reputation for reforming preconceived notions of window display, she was brought in to head the BBC's newly created Studio Design Unit, in charge of settings for the Talks Department. The successful use of 'good design', in such programmes as the aforementioned *Joan Gilbert's Diary*, had demonstrated that this type of production was particularly suitable for contemporary settings. Kroll has stated that she was specifically employed for her 'taste' and her particular 'knowledge of display, contemporary retail and foreign design'.[19] These influences could be strongly discerned in television settings of the period, and their interrelationship was demonstrated by the use of textured flats, translucent or partially obscured screens, photomontage, fabrics, plants and contemporary furniture (see Figure 8.3).

By the middle of the decade, post-war restrictions were being phased out and furniture and consumer goods were increasingly available for studio settings. The type of furniture and furnishings used were 'pieces that were universal, anything that was well designed', the most important feature was that it looked 'handsome and tasteful' and that it did not 'intrude' in any way.[20] The BBC was fortunate that it did not have to purchase contemporary products from manufacturers and retailers. Discerning designers with money to spend encouraged the growth of furniture-hire firms around Television Centre so that the BBC could rely on a steady flow of recently manufactured furniture. Levin also began to use interviews and advertisements within trade magazines appealing to British furniture manufacturers to produce more ranges of 'good design' for utilisation within television. He pointed out that the television screen should act as a showcase for new ideas saying: 'television is like an exhibition ... you don't want everyday stuff on the screen. You want to be a step ahead and excite interest'.[21]

The work of the Studio Design Unit became the most important part of the Design Department's output essentially because it allowed the viewers a window into the 'home' of the Corporation. The consistent use of modern furniture and furnishings within these studio settings lent what was believed to be a progressive atmosphere to television's output, an atmosphere intended to reflect the tastes and thinking of the BBC itself. The use of the modern idiom was to become indispensable for the BBC, a factor thoroughly consolidated by the arrival of commercial television in September 1955. The end of the BBC's monopoly and the arrival of independent television played a fundamental role in the substantiation of the television designer's profession. Before the emergence of competition, everything the Corporation had done was contained within a vacuum in which it alone designated what television, as a medium, might be and how it should be presented. The commercial imperatives of the rival channels immediately positioned television firmly within sceptical post-war discourses surrounding the effects of mass culture and questions of social decay and decline.

8.3 *The Edge of Success* designed by Natasha Kroll, circa 1956.

From the beginning, those who saw themselves as custodians of British culture had found it difficult to accept radio broadcasting, let alone television, as the pervasive nature of these forms of mass communication was seen to be levelling down culture. This cultural unease informed the BBC's emphasis on its aesthetics. The BBC designers themselves became an important element within a battle to counteract and claim the moral high ground over commercialisation and elevate the profile of the electronic medium. The Studio Design Unit in particular was used to forge a hierarchical position for the BBC. Its designers' previous training, in architectural and exhibition work, practices that were equally involved with the projection of aspirational ideals, ensured their proficiency at incorporating visual prestige into their work. The utilisation of 'good design' was therefore not only rooted in the national, moral and aesthetic ideology of design reform, but was also driven by a moral responsibility to raise the cultural standing and integrity of the medium both as a whole and as a publicly funded service.

Early soap opera and the contemporary style

In 1956, the success of the modern idiom, particularly within the year-old Studio Design Unit and a limited number of one-off dramas, encouraged the Department to try to take 'good design' into a bastion of British television drama: *The Grove Family*. This was an early soap opera, based around the life and times of a lower-middle-class family as they became immersed in 'a variety of social situations and consumer concerns'.[22] In Bernard Hollowood's scathing attack on television design, he described *The Grove Family* as 'domesticated in an aura of lower-middle class respectability with a living room of left-overs from a Victorian jumble sale'.[23] *The Grove Family* offered an authentic picture of home and family in a Britain still bound up with post-war austerity. The initial scripts designated that the house should look 'shabby',[24] in order to represent a life that lower-middle-class and working-class viewers could identify with, rather than to offer a source of domestic and social aspiration.

The Design Department felt that since so many people watched *The Grove Family* there could be no better platform from which to preach the doctrine of 'good design'. An opportunity came in June of that year, when the actors visited the Council of Industrial Design's newly opened Design Centre. This publicity stunt was Levin's idea, part of a policy of acceptable advertising for the Council who were to loan furniture of 'advanced design' for the programme's new settings. This was the next phase, to rid this famous family of what Levin described as its 'middle class slum atmosphere'.[25] He got the screenwriters to alter the script by using the simple expedient of a fire that destroyed the Groves's home and furniture. The son of the family, who had fortunately just come back from art school, then took charge of the redecorating. This manipulation of the script allowed the incorporation of 'good design' into the programme, yet the project was to prove disastrous from the start. Immediately after the first episode to feature the newly decorated set, John Warrington, the director of the series, wrote to the BBC's management to complain that the decor did not create what he considered to be an 'actuality' background.

> The design is negative. No warmth, unlived in and unloved. In fact, not the home of a pleasant middle aged lower-middle class suburban

family of four children and a great grand mother. The best description given to me so far is 'a young newly married civil service clerk trying to be Mayfair on £8 a week'. It does look like any Woman's Hour or utility interview programme setting ... the BBC is in 'the middle of an important question, will design control production or production control design in the overall picture required by the programme content ... What is to be done. I enclose a copy of House and Garden, December. Incidentally the before and after pictures were supplied by the Head of Television Design![26]

Warrington asked for various alterations beginning with the Heal and Sons dining table and Gordon Russell chairs, suggesting that they be darkened to a heavy oak colour to make them look more 'solid and homely'. Secondly that the fireplace breast be covered in dark wallpaper as its lightness, alongside the furniture was not 'agreeable with the technicalities of the studio's lighting'. It continued with a demand that the Hille settee and armchair be replaced with a less austere design, something more 'comfortable' in shape and covered in 'chintz'.[27] Even the properties were criticised for their inauthenticity. Warrington suggested that the table lamp and fire irons be replaced and that calendars, pictures and ornaments be added, so it appeared as though a family actually lived in the setting.

In his written response Levin was conciliatory. He accepted that the set did look rather bleak, suggesting that the changes be done in stages so as not to create a sense of confusion in the eyes of the viewers. He agreed with all the suggestions except the first item of which he commented:

> I do not think darkening the furniture will really have the effect of making it more 'solid' but would, in fact, only tend to make it look 'Dragey'. It is certainly not in the public interest to promote this kind of furniture in the home and I am sure that if you can reconcile the light furniture with the programme it will be a good thing all round.[28]

The before and after pictures of the setting supplied to the editor of *House and Garden* have ensured that this particular programme has been registered and commented upon within design history, as an important example of 'good design' within television in the 1950s.[29] However, this representation is inaccurate because the implementation

8.4 The set of the popular television drama *The Grove Family*, 1956.

of contemporary design into this setting was notable for being one of the BBC Design Departments' greatest failures. Before the Groves's home was made over into a model of the new style, the programme had consistently achieved high television ratings. Following viewer disappointment with the new setting, the programme was removed from the schedule within three weeks, as the audience stopped watching.

The viewers' dislike of the new home suggests that it did not correspond with their expectations, ruining the programme's continuity along with its audience's enjoyment of and commitment to the series. The failure of this venture is obvious in a still from the show (see Figure 8.4). The characters seem incongruous and uncomfortable, as though they have been placed in an exhibition show room. It is not difficult to see a general principle here, namely that contemporary design within television settings functioned so long as it contributed to the passage of relevant information to the viewer. In a studio setting, modern design could be pleasantly and successfully preached because the viewer was not asked to identify him or herself with the background. As the problems encountered with the Grove's set have demonstrated, the information needed for successful drama design depended on specific and recognisable detail and not on any elite notions of 'good taste'.

The BBC Design Department: tastemakers to the nation?

Previously in December 1956, the *Cabinet Maker and Complete House Furnisher* had analysed whether the 'visual appeal' of television design was directing the general public toward a 'contemporary mindedness' and concluded that it was having a 'steady and un-dramatic infiltration' into the viewer's sensibilities.[30] It is correct to say that the contemporary styling within television played a role in disseminating the new look to a mass market. Nevertheless, an exact definition of its influence on the taste of the nation is difficult to ascertain. The BBC certainly played a part in the acceptance of the style – even new wallpapers behind broadcasters' heads would inspire requests from viewers asking where they could be purchased. But though undeniably influential, this was only one aspect of the machinery of mass communication that projected similar ideologies in the 1950s. As Leslie Kleeman, the Design Supply Organiser of the BBC, pointed out in 1960, 'my desk is stacked with viewers letters asking where we got the pattern and furniture … where can I find an armchair like the one so and so was murdered in'.[31]

It was Levin's conviction that, in the first ten years he worked in the service, television design, most specifically in the form of studio backgrounds, did in fact stimulate public understanding and acceptance of 'good design'. The anecdote he frequently related, as confirmation of his influence on the public's taste and buying habits, concerns an incident, from 1955, when the BBC began its transmissions in Scotland. At this time he held a conversation with the Chairman of the Scottish Furniture Manufacturers Association, who told him that before the arrival of television the only furniture selling in Dundee was solid and bulbous 'Mock-Jacobean'. This was to change however within weeks of the service opening, as his retail outlet received inquiries for the contemporary furniture that appeared in the BBC's broadcasts and within months he responded by adapting his entire stock.[32]

It is interesting that in 1955, the press coverage of the Earls Court British Furniture Exhibition appeared to offer a correlation to Levin's assertions. This annual trade show had 285 manufacturers displaying their wares; it was a particularly traditional exhibition with 'stand after stand of resplendent over stuffed Victorian monstrosities in heady rich crimsons'.[33] Media reports indicated however that on closer inspection,

among the mass of traditional furniture, there was a good deal that was
of contemporary design, more examples in fact than had been exhibited
in any of the five previous years.

> It is the talk of the furniture trade that a number of television
> programmes this winter which depicted contemporary furniture
> have stimulated an immediate and considerable demand for this sort
> of design in areas which have hitherto remained obstinately mid-
> Victorian. There is some nervous talk that the coming of competitive
> television may accelerate this trend, if more and more contemporary
> designs are to be seen by a vast nightly audience.[34]

Within a consideration of how far television promoted the contemporary style, it must be recognised that its use may not have achieved
the desired effect on popular taste. The grey tones of this monochrome
medium inevitably removed the vivid colour that was one of contemporary design's essential humanising factors. Also, by harnessing the
modern idiom for its corporate image, the BBC may have endowed the
style with a public, undomesticated character. Both of these aspects
may have reinforced the public's perception of its modern aesthetic as
uncomfortable and alien, rather than generating its popular acceptance
in the private sphere. The use of contemporary furnishings was a specific
attempt to enthral the audience on a psychological level to accept the
hidden message of the 'good design' ethos. This style was absorbed
into the visual image of the BBC, yet there is no reason to assume that
the viewers adopted these ideals. The consistent use of contemporary
furniture and furnishings within television's backgrounds may have
allowed the spirit of this neo-modernism to be passively received
without an understanding of its underlying principles. In this way,
television's reliance on this style may have contributed to the well-
documented vulgarisation of contemporary design over the course of
the decade.

By the beginning of the 1960s, the use of the 'good design' canon
had become a system particular to BBC studio settings: a form of
expression to justify its social position and validate the medium by
negating its role as an instrument of mass communication and culture.
Neo-modernism became a visual monolith in the television design of
the 1950s that was to guide, control and form the pioneering practice

of television design. However, in the following decade it began to lose its hegemony, as the aesthetics of popular culture came to the fore, undermining the established ideal of 'good taste'. Nevertheless its institution within the Design Department of the BBC was to remain as an underlying philosophy. The new values of youth culture slowly permeated what came to be seen as the 'stuffy' house style of the BBC, and this displacement was to be furthered and solidified by the advancement of television technology and the arrival of colour in 1969.

Notes

1 H. Hopkins, *The New Look: A Social History of the Forties and Fifties in Britain* (London: Secker & Warburg, 1963), p. 331.

2 Richard Levin was Head of the BBC Design Department between 1953 and 1971. Paper by R. Levin presented at the 'International Television Design Conference on behalf of the European Broadcasting Union', London, 7 May 1962.

3 John Reith quoted in P. Black, *The Mirror in the Corner* (London: Hutchinson of London, 1972), p. 76.

4 Internal Memo, 4 May 1945, 'From Mr. Hilton Brown. Subject: CoID Features', Council of Industrial Design Files, BBC Written Archive Centre, Reading, Berkshire, UK.

5 Ibid. Internal BBC Letter, 4 December 1950. 'From: P. Thompson, To: Mary Adams (Head of Talks) Subject: 'Furniture for Picture Page.'

6 Ibid. Internal BBC Memo, 17 April 1954, 'From: Richard Levin (Head of Television Design) To Cecil McGivern (Head of Television Programming) Subject: The Design Department'.

7 *The Times*, 5 March 1953, 'Appointment of Richard Levin aged 42'.

8 Although the influence of inter-war European design on Levin is crucial, many people like Reyner Banham and those writing for the *Architectural Review* believed that a unique form of English modernism was also making itself felt during this period. This style was more attuned to the landscape and was sometimes described as more 'feminine' than Continental modernism. Such debates emerged particularly in relation to the 1951 Festival of Britain, on which many of the protagonists in this chapter actually worked (two examples being Misha Black and Ernest Race). For further discussion of the Festival and its significant role in defining contemporary British design and taste see M. Banham

and B. Hillier, *A Tonic to the Nation: The Festival of Britain, 1951* (London: Thames & Hudson, 1976) and B.E. Conekin, *The Autobiography of a Nation: The 1951 Festival of Britain* (Manchester and New York: Manchester University Press, 2003).

9   Internal BBC Memo, 5 July 1949, 'From: Peter Bax (Head of Design and Supply) To: Cecil McGivern (Head of Television Programming)' BBC Written Archive Centre.

10 Ibid. R. Levin, *Television and Design* BBC Lunchtime Lectures, Series Seven, 3–11 December 1968, BBC Written Archive Centre.

11 N. Kroll interviewed by the author, 6 November 1998.

12 R. Levin interviewed by the author, 26 January 1999.

13 Ibid.

14 B. Hollowood, 'On the Air TV in 3D', *Punch*, 2 May 1956.

15 Internal Memo, 10 March 1955. 'From: R. Levin To: the Controller of Programming. 'Subject: Nominations for outside design contracts". BBC Written Archive Centre.

16 Clifford Hatts took over from Richard Levin as Head of Design when Levin retired in 1975.

17 The Festival of Britain was held from May to September 1951 at the South Bank, London.

18 *Design*, March 1952, p. 26.

19 N. Kroll interviewed by the author, 6 November 1998.

20 Ibid.

21 *Cabinet Maker and Complete House Furnisher*, 29 December 1956.

22 Grove Family Script. Episode one, 9 April 1954, BBC Written Archive Centre.

23 B. Hollowood, 'On the Air TV in 3D', *Punch*, 2 May 1956.

24 Ibid. Grove Family Script. Episode one. 9 April 1954.

25 R. Levin, *Furniture Record*, 29 June 1956.

26 Internal Memo. 29 November 1956 'From: John Warrington. To: Head of Television Design. Subject: Grove Family Set.' BBC Written Archive Centre.

27 Ibid. Internal Memo. 29 November 1956 'From: John Warrington. To: Head of Television Design. Subject: Grove Family Set.'

28 Ibid. Internal Memo. 30 November 1956. 'From: Head of Television Design To: Head of Light Entertainment. Subject: Grove Family.'

29 G. Robyns, 'Design on Television', *House and Garden* 11(12) (96), December

1956, pp. 41–2. Perhaps significantly, the editor of this magazine was Natasha Kroll's brother.

30 *Cabinet Maker and Complete House Furnisher,* 29 December, 1956.

31 E. Thomson, 'You never see a studio wall', *Radio Times,* October 1960.

32 R. Levin, 'Television and Design', BBC Lunchtime Lectures, 7th Series, 3–11 December 1968, p. 14. BBC Written Archive Centre.

33 *Manchester Guardian,* 15 February 1955.

34 Ibid.

9 ✧ The evolution of a new televisual language: the sets, title sequences and consumers of *Ready Steady Go!* 1963–1966

Alice Twemlow

Ready Steady Go! was a television pop-music programme that captured the spirit of a period and transmitted the consciousness of a generation – visually, aurally and emotionally.[1] From the date of its first broadcast at 7.00 pm on 9 August 1963 to its demise on 23 December 1966, the programme was poised on the pinnacle of Pop.

The dates of *RSG!*'s rise and fall coincide with the era that historian Nigel Whiteley has identified as 'high Pop'.[2] This three-year period saw the most concentrated expression of the attitudes and concerns of a nascent British youth culture to date. It was also the culmination of a more protracted domestication of European Modernism and its cultural imperatives. With its distinctive music, set design and title sequences, *RSG!* provided a unique space for the convergence of an intellectual renegotiation of Modernist design on the part of its creators and the immediate responses to the intensified condition of modernity on the part of its targeted teenage audience.

While *RSG!*'s mission was neither satirical nor political, the pop programme was certainly part of a larger, and specifically generational, anti-establishment movement.[3] In a precarious balance that lasted three years, it fused the preoccupations of a rebellious and elitist Avant-garde with aspects of modern unselfconscious popular culture in a configuration that transgressed deep-set divisions between the elite and the mass, creative production and passive consumption.

New producers, new consumers

By 1963, when *RSG!* was first broadcast, the pop-music show existed as a format distinct from other light-entertainment productions on British television. With the growth of the record industry during the 1950s and the compilation of the charts on the basis of record sales, rather than of sheet music, pop-record-based radio programmes flourished. It was not long before the BBC and the new independent television companies began to exploit the potential of this genre through a succession of programmes.

These programmes were modelled on the experience of a big-band concert and used the conventions of the music hall. Transmitted at teatime on Saturday, they were aimed at a family audience. Yet still they incited critics' fears about the effects on the young of manipulative and distasteful American pop music. For example, in 1960, The Council for Children's Welfare issued a report on early-evening television programming that included a section devoted to the permissive attitudes and values espoused by the ten BBC and nine ITV music and variety shows on the air at that time:

> Both TV channels now run weekly programmes in which popular records are played to teenagers and judged. While the music is performed the cameras linger savagely over the faces of the audience. What a bottomless chasm of vacuity they reveal. Huge faces, bloated with cheap confectionery and smeared with chain-store make up, the open sagging mouths and glazed eyes, the hands mindlessly drumming in time to the music, the broken stiletto heels, the shoddy, stereotyped 'with it' clothes: here, apparently, is a collective portrait of a generation enslaved by a commercial machine.[4]

While belonging to this condemned class of programming, *RSG!* was dissimilar from its predecessors and competitors in several key respects. No attempts were made to disguise the fact that the pop programme was broadcast from a television studio: cameras emblazoned with the *RSG!* logo were nearly always in shot, as were its cameramen, technicians and floor managers. All the elements instrumental to the generation of a television image were revealed in what amounted to a celebration of modern communications technology. *RSG!* then, in a spectacular fusion of sound and image, its material and its means, can be seen to have crystallised a broader tendency among the practitioners of Pop to achieve simultaneity in the creation of surface and meaning.

Elkan Allen, the head of Associated Rediffusion's entertainment department, was *RSG!*'s executive producer, and his role highlights the ambivalent relationship between control and spontaneity that characterised the programme. Despite efforts to model himself upon more genuine pop magnates such as Phil Spector, described by Tom Wolfe, as 'the first tycoon of teen', a generation divided the 42-year-old Allen from his audience and, as executive producer, his interest in the programme was commercial rather than personal.[5] Other members of the team, however, especially certain directors of the show including Michael Lindsay-Hogg, and the teenagers Vicki Wickham, Michael Aldred and Cathy McGowan, could claim a much closer affinity with the idiosyncratic spirit of the programme and the fickle musical preferences of its audience.[6]

RSG! fed directly from the sexually liberated demeanours of urban American blues singers and the British bands that emulated them. An *RSG!* viewer remembers that 'all the most interesting performers appeared, their presentation was more direct and aggressive, less condescending and diluted with easy listening than that of other pop programmes'.[7] The use of American stars such as The Supremes, James Brown and Otis Redding, seemed to fly in the face of the Establishment, epitomised by the BBC, where the Postmaster General had issued a ban on US records.[8] 'For me, its glory was the music', says another viewer of the programme. 'Live performances by Charles and Inez Foxx, Eric Burden ... *RSG!* offered the best selection on TV, reflecting what was really "in" and aimed at a young audience.'[9]

Cathy McGowan, of Streatham, began as teenage adviser to the programme and went on to become its co-host. She endeared herself through her frequent mistakes that verified her genuineness to a viewing audience of urban and suburban working-class teenagers. She became *Melody Maker*'s female personality of the year in its 1965 pop poll. Her social mobility mirrored the rise of pop stars from anonymity to stardom that composer and music critic Frank Cordell described:

> The transition from 'unknown' to 'star' takes place in that vague area where the common myth is shared: Although our garage-hand is now

a 'star' he is still an 'available' type identifiable with the mass and as his press agent will underline, he still retains the tastes and allegiances of his group.[10]

In their role as comperes, Cathy and Keith Fordyce introduced each group and their songs, sometimes in combination with a quick interview. 'When they hired me as compere for *RSG!*', wrote Fordyce in the 1964 *RSG! Annual*, 'they told me to keep it moving faster than any show there had ever been … interviews hardly ever last for longer than a minute.'[11]

The directors endeavoured to eliminate any sense of distinction between star and fan, stage and audience. 'There was no great agitation or excitement about seeing the performers – they would do their set and then dance in the audience', recalls a viewer. Singers had to walk through the crowds and, when they did stand on rostra that were scattered about the studio, their heads were only just cleared for the cameras. Most other pop shows kept their performers, quite literally, on pedestals, and their well-behaved audiences seated. Elkan Allen's decision to decrease the reliance on miming, in 1965, also accentuated the raw performance of the singer. Allen believed that 'seeing a mimed show – and the BBC still puts them out – is like hearing music through plate glass'.[12]

The audience members in the *RSG!* studio were as much a part of the show as the performers; their clothes, gestures, poses and dances were integral to the design of the programme. Derek Boshier and Pauline Boty, two of the artists featured in Ken Russell's 1962 TV film *Pop Goes the Easel*, often danced in the audience. Mostly, dancers were carefully selected from clubs such as The Scene, on Great Windmill Street (well known for its choice of bands and its play-list of rare American records) by the production team who informally auditioned teenagers for their dancing ability and fashion sense.

RSG!'s most avid followers were teenagers known as mods.[13] Discerning and narcissistic, these working-class teenagers were readily identified by their closely cropped hairstyles and meticulously tailored outfits, and lived mainly in London and the New Towns in the South. Among the main foci of expenditure among this new demographic were records, hair styling and clothes. Wearing the right clothes with the right cut, from the right tailors, was a fundamental prerequisite for being a mod. Being knowledgeable about a particular fashion, initiated by a stylist and which may have only lasted for a week, necessitated a rapidity of dissemination that a weekly television programme like *RSG!* certainly helped to achieve.

Mod appropriation of clothing was largely related to the subtle art of body management. Tablets of drynamil cost around 6d each (85p at today's prices) and were sold in brown envelopes or wage packets. This hard currency of amphetamine increased the heart rate, enlarged the pupils and contributed to an angularity of stance and over-alertness that fed new non-partner, mod-specific dances such as 'The Block.'

Dancing was only one aspect of the mod body language that could be read from the audiences of *RSG!* There were specific poses, codes of gesture and walks which were more subtle, but essential to the overall image. Photographers such as Terrance Donovan, David Bailey and Brian Duffy would go to London's East End to observe the design of movement among teenagers.[14] In an article entitled 'Gesture Goes Classless,' pop critic George Melly identified a detached coolness and 'anti-elegance' among the young, transmitted through photography in magazines and television that could cut across social boundaries and class barriers but not across generational ones.[15]

The RSG studio space

From 1964 onward, the background flats in the studio where *RSG!* was filmed were designed by Nicholas Ferguson, a graduate of Chelsea School of Art and of Painting and Theatre Design at the Slade. When executive producer Elkan Allen explained his vision for the way the programme should look ('He wanted it to look un-designed') Ferguson realised he would be able to draw on his own experience and interests, derived from high culture rather than the street.[16] 'I knew completely what he meant because of my theatre experience, my knowledge of Brecht and his rejection of stage illusion', recalls Ferguson.[17] Ferguson, who saw the Royal Shakespeare Company's groundbreaking English production of *The Caucasian Chalk Circle* in 1962, employed Brechtian-infused techniques to draw attention to the artificiality of the stage and auditorium – an approach that was still novel in British theatrical set design.[18]

The minimal nature of *RSG!*'s set design, however, was informed as much by economic necessity as it was by the ideological and aesthetic preferences of its creator. Ferguson's predecessor had exhausted the production budget, leaving a restrictive weekly allowance of £13.12 shillings (in today's values £456). Ferguson found that certain scenic devices, such as painted backcloths, were not charged to his budget.[19] He used these cloths to create dynamic collages, finding his inspiration in mainstream Neo-Dadaist artists such as Robert Rauschenberg and Dada collagists such as Kurt Schwitters.[20] Ferguson's collages were made using typographic and photographic fragments torn from newspapers and a profusion of new pop magazines such as *Teen Beat, Pop Shop, Fabulous, New Musical Express* and *Pop Weekly.*

Ferguson's approach to collage epitomises a renegotiation of the philosophy and practice of collage, montage and assemblage that was popular in 1960s Britain. The Dadaist and Cubist deployment of brutally torn and roughly cut fragments of paper had been charged with a political and moral purpose specific to their historical context. Collage provided a shared visual idiom for these artists to express some of the anxiety and excitement of the experience of rapid urbanisation and industrialisation in early twentieth-century Europe, as well as a means to make political critique.[21] By the early 1960s, however, the political resonances of collage were diluted. Polish poet and publisher Stefan Themerson described it thus:

> Modern Collage is not much interested in what its materials were before, nor where they came from. If it is photos of Brigitte Bardot etc. this is because BB has some mythological significance for the Sixties – no more. Most people would be able to read Schwitters as 'innocent aesthetic arrangements' because in the 60s surely, ANTI-ART has finished: the personal protest has finished ... anti-art is third programme material.[22]

If the original purpose and meaning of collage was consigned to the dusty halls of high culture – the old guard of BBC radio programming – as Themerson suggests, then the aesthetic potential of the art form was wide open for investigation by a new breed of depoliticised artists, designers and typographers working in the commercial sphere.

The autonomy of the individual artist was, even at Rediffusion, tempered to some extent by its administrative agencies. Ferguson had not realised that the photographs he was manipulating were subject to such legal niceties such as copyright and, once the company lawyer spotted this aberration, Ferguson was forced to use more staid publicity stills obtained from the artists' agents, those that, in Frank Cordell's words, 'generally show (the performer) leaning out of the frame extending the glad hand and big smile to the consumers, or posed in an attitude that unambiguously invites adulation'.[23] To avoid this restriction, and to achieve a surface and texture that evoked Pop, Ferguson began to rely more heavily upon typographic samples in his collages. In ways that prefigured an increasingly interdependent relationship between the hitherto discrete activities of set design and title design, Ferguson used pieces of artwork, such as the logo for *RSG!*, produced in the graphic-design department. The interdisciplinary exchange was reinforced when the title-sequence designers used Ferguson's sets for subject matter and even their construction process.

The artwork Ferguson completed at the beginning of each week was photographed, enlarged and pasted onto flats measuring 10 by 8 feet, ready for transmission that Friday evening. Each week new montages would be wallpapered over the last like posters on an advertising hoarding. Ferguson remembers 'the smell of those flats and their thickness after a while'.[24] Their ephemeral nature signalled Pop, and so did the immediacy of their content; topical elements could be added up until the last minute. The week before the Parliamentary election, the face of Sir Alec Douglas Home appeared crowned by a Beatles haircut made from a spaghetti advertisement, for example. And once, the Associated Rediffusion lawyer made Ferguson paint out his depiction of an atom-bomb explosion which was to provide the backdrop for a performance of the song 'Here Comes the Rain' even while the programme was on air. By extracting 'a replaceable, expendable series of ikons' from magazines and newspapers, Ferguson was dealing with the very substance of mass media, which was again reproduced by the television cameras.[25] Thus he was participating as both a producer and a consumer of mass communications.

Ferguson's flats – painted in black and white, with the notable exception of signal red which had a grey tonal equivalent when filmed in monochrome and was purely for the benefit of the studio audience,

technicians and performers – were intended to be glimpsed periph-
erally. 'The paintings are only supposed to be seen quickly in the
background,' explained Ferguson in the 1964 *RSG Annual*. 'I just aim to
get shapes and symbols that are relevant to a Pop programme.'[26]

RSG! belonged to a breed of scenography that was idiosyncratic
in many respects. It was not part of the tasteful design revolution
that, since the mid-1950s, Richard Levin had been leading at the BBC;
neither did it find a direct counterpart among independent television's
other pop-music shows, characterised by their gestalt Pop emblems and
streamlining. When Ferguson says of Tony Borer, the designer at *Top of
the Pops*, 'He was the forerunner of the type of design that is still going
with its cyclorama shapes; mine is not still going', he intimates that a
true visual realisation of Pop such as his own would never have had
such staying power.[27]

Ferguson tried to reflect the type of music being played visually,
demonstrating a painterly concern with patterns, textures and tones
of surface. The 'difficulty of resolving images created in the mind
through hearing, and the associations which are formed by a purely
visual stimulus'[28] that Levin perceived provided Ferguson with what he
regarded as an 'intellectual challenge.' His blown-up flats, tailor-made
to fit the featured stars of each week's show, contained visual references,
incongruities, puns and resonances that simultaneously celebrated and
satirised, reassured and confused.

When subjected to the two-dimensional format of the television
screen, the featured pop stars became interchangeable components
with their own pictorial and photographic representations on the
montaged sets behind them. Sound design, too, played its part in this
newly ambiguous relationship between foreground and background.
Frank Cordell noted that, by using a microphone, 'a singer's voice is
brought well forward in the sound perspective, on a separate plane
to the accompaniment. This effect of aural close up, like its visual
counterpart in movies, enables the audience the pleasure of the
performer's presence'.[29]

Even more disjunctive than the lacerated textural flats used in
RSG!, then, was the way in which the programme was filmed to reveal
the structure of the studio and the technologies of its transmission.
George Melly coined the term 'new telly brutalism' to describe the

situation where the technical artillery of cameras and lighting along with their operators were casually in evidence.[30]

Four cameras were used in the transmission of the programme. The introduction of the zoom lens had revolutionised television broadcast by allowing the same camera to track the action while zooming in on it. Bill Metcalfe, one of *RSG!*'s cameramen, was responsible for experimenting with staggered 8:1 zooms which captured the beat of the music, like a visual equivalent of electronic feedback.[31]

The language of close-up shots was unfamiliar to television viewers in the early 1960s. Performers were more usually seen as mid-shot busts. *RSG!*'s confrontational presentation of singers, therefore, seemed to aptly reflect the raw energy of the music being played. It corresponded more with the techniques used in films such as Dick Lester's 1964 film *A Hard Days Night* – that, according to George Melly, 'altered the whole concept of how to deal with pop on both film and television'.[32]

The mediation of imagery via the close-up can be seen as a metaphor for a widespread shift in relation to visual technology on the part of the consumer. As the 'long front of culture'[33] extended, the ideal of a 'critical distance' began to erode. Viewers were able to confront and to immerse themselves in imagery – a phenomenon excitedly evoked by Marshall McLuhan: 'in television, images are projected at you. You are the screen. The images wrap around you. You are the vanishing point'.[34]

Kinetic graphics

The graphic-design department at Associated Rediffusion afforded its designers great freedom. Michael Yates, head of the department from 1956 to 1968, aimed to create a space in which designers could operate to their fullest potential, free from the constraints of administration and bureaucracy. Like his mentor Richard Levin at the BBC, Yates believed in creating 'a state of organised anarchy' in which the 'freedom of the individual is not hampered'.[35]

In August 1960, the German magazine *Gebrauchsgraphik* devoted eight pages to the programme promotion cards produced by the graphic-design department at Rediffusion, concluding that 'In all these designs the television graphic designers show an outstanding

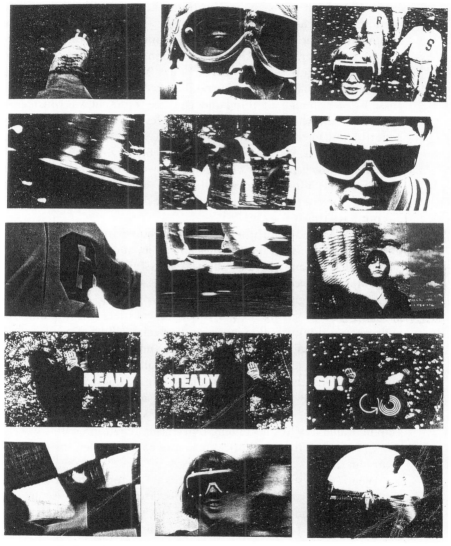

9.1 Stills from 'My Generation' sequence from *Ready Steady Go!* designed by Arnold Schwartzman, 1965.

originality which probably results from the unusually great artistic freedom which they are granted',[36] a view which is reinforced by the designers' memories of their informal working environment. When Arnold Schwartzman directed a live-action skateboarding sequence for *RSG!* (see Figure 9.1), cut to The Who's 'My Generation', he edited the footage so that the images would succeed one another as fast as possible, even though anything under a three-frame cut was considered subliminal and therefore illegal by the Television Act of 1964.[37] It is doubtful how forcefully such a rule would have been observed, as none of the designers at Rediffusion could remember having a title sequence turned down by a producer or director. Schwartzman recalls a 'strange freedom', and Sidney King says that '[d]irectors would only look at things just before transmission. Even if they didn't like something they did not have time to say no'.[38]

The Associated Rediffusion music-services department was situated on the same floor as the graphic-design studio, and well out of earshot of 'the bridge', from where ex-naval captain Tom Brownrigg managed the company. Clive Arrowsmith, a young designer, would play the new releases unceasingly as he worked on the programme's title sequences (see Figure 9.2). Among the graphic designers there was a familiarity with, and sensitivity to, pop music, and especially the distinctive sound of new British Beat and American Rhythm and Blues and Motown, that enabled the titles to embody most emphatically both the essence of the programme and the visual, social and cultural concerns of an era. In their search for new modes of graphic expression suited to such sounds, the designers sought recourse to an eclectic spectrum of film, art and graphic influences in the contemporary visual environment as well as those plundered from a historical reference bank of styles, imagery and techniques.

When *RSG!*'s surviving title sequences are arranged chronologically, an evolution of content and form is discernible. The title sequences made in 1963 and 1964 tend to embody a sensibility and references derived from the practice of magazine art direction; while those from the latter years of the programme reflect their creators' increasing involvement in film direction.[39]

A sequence crudely animated with a Rostrum bench camera to the specially commissioned Manfred Mann tune '5,4,3,2,1,' of late

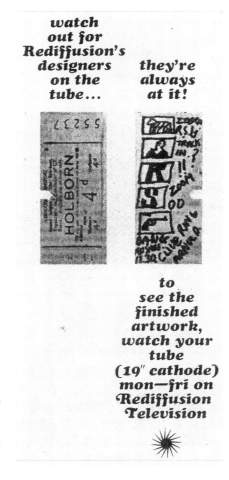

watch
out for
Rediffusion's
designers
on the   they're
tube...   always
                   at it!

to
see the
finished
artwork,
watch your
tube
(19″ cathode)
mon—fri on
Rediffusion
Television

9.2 Advertisement designed by
Arnold Schwartzman using Clive
Arrowsmith's tube-ticket sketches
for a sequence that features a
zebra, 1965.

1963 represents a realisation and extension of the kinetic potential of
the magazine medium in two ways. First, the speed of the staggered
zoom toward the letterforms increases in parallel to the rising tempo
of the music until the words fill the whole screen and burst beyond
its framing capacity, furthering the explosiveness of full-bleed in
a print context. Secondly, the title sequence accelerates the activity
of turning over the sequenced pages in a magazine. Tom Wolsey's
syncopated pagination of *Town*, for example, juxtaposed pictorially

9.3 Stills from 'Hubble Bubble' sequence designed by Clive Arrowsmith, 1964.

and typographically dominated layouts and carried elements across the page turn.[40]

Furthermore, the experience of watching a television set of the period was a conscious act. With its poor reception and 405-line resolution, the set would have functioned less as a window for viewers to look through, and more as a frame for the mosaic mesh of ceaselessly scanning dots to be looked at.

Another Rostrum-animated sequence, used during the summer of 1964 and underscored by another Manfred Mann tune, 'Hubble Bubble,' reveals a more sophisticated interaction with screen space than before (see Figure 9.3). The screen is treated less as an editorial spread, in which photographs and illustrations are manipulated, and more as a selected viewpoint in a continuous field of action. It provides a marked contrast with the traditional methods of lettering and use of centred caption cards that had characterised graphic design for television since its inception, and that were still widely practised. Graphic activity tended to be confined to what the television design manuals called the 'safety area' – originally necessitated by the poor quality of television reception and perpetuated by producers who sent requisition forms to the designers with lists of credit information neatly typed and squarely centred.

The sequence presents the face of a woman moving on horizontal and diagonal axes and then beyond the limits of the framed white space. The movement is so fast that the black of her hair leaves a strobe-like trail in the wake of each swishing movement. 'Strobing', as defined and discouraged by The Guild of TV Producers and Directors in *The Grammar of TV Production* 1966, is 'a streaking juddering effect caused by the camera and the subject moving too fast in relation to one another'.[41]

The face comes to rest in the centre of the screen and a new working surface is created by the camera zooming in to the simple Op-art forms of a pair of circular sunglasses. A selection of bizarre and incongruent Victorian engravings appears in succession upon the circular lenses. The images – which the sequence's designer Schwartzman sampled from the Weaver Smith collection of engravings, that, from 1961 onward, was situated in Rediffusion's library adjacent to the design department on the fourth floor – can be seen as part of a widespread revival of interest in Victoriana within many areas of art and design production and consumption at this time.⁴² This non-reverential sampling of Victorian artefacts and ephemera for surreal effect is probably best exemplified by Terry Gilliam's graphics for the BBC Television *Monty Python* series in 1969, and was part of a larger impetus in which the iconography of the Imperial past and an absurd renegotiation of militaria was used to satirise the Establishment.

A title sequence produced in the summer of 1966 marks a departure in content and form, not only from the genre of contemporary television title sequences but also from those that had been used to introduce *RSG!* to date. While the early sequences celebrate surface (through use of archetypal pop symbols such as the target), this one introduces a more hallucinatory vision of reality, beginning to show the influences of Psychedelia and the questioning impulse of an emergent Underground. It features two pieces of film – one a piece of archival footage of jitter-bugging dancers and the other of Cathy McGowan shot in a pastoral location – cut to the soul track 'Land of 1,000 Dances' by Wilson Pickett on Atlantic Records. Instead of the profusion of pop images that charac-terised previous sequences, this one is minimalist in its concentration upon a limited range of repeated shots and images creating patterns, redolent of experimental film of the 1920s. Jump cuts that disrupt the continuity of Cathy's turning head resonate with an informality of direction and movement associated with the use of hand-held camera work, found in the French Nouvelle Vague films of Jean-Luc Godard and François Truffaut. Additionally, the use of high and low angles rather than a reliance on centred shots implies the director was seeing with a cinematic rather than a graphic eye.

The content and messages of this sequence, too, mark a distinct shift in mood from that of earlier sequences. This change is played out in a concentrated form through a conflict between two oppositional modes of behaviour. Cathy is shown as passive, fluid and trance-like, repeatedly covering her face with her hands. Interspersed with these shots are scenes of jitterbuggers who are energetic, angular and excitable. She is shown sitting in a field, a possible reference to the emergence of student 'sit-ins' as a form of political protest. Her location may also suggest a rejection of the values implicit in a consumerist, materialist Western society, values that had been celebrated, or at least promoted emphatically, in previous title sequences. Her silent scream is suggestive of the fine line between dream and nightmare, good and bad trip, the 'nyktomorph' of Christopher Booker's *The Neophiliacs*.[43] It hints at some great and unseen horror such as the atrocities of the Vietnam war, and presages a retreat into meditational silence and an exploration of the inner spaces of time, memory and imagination that would dominate the next phase of 1960s visual production.

The transition, traced within these *RSG!* title sequences, from a reliance on a graphically orientated idiom to an exploration of a filmic medium, reflects the way in which the preoccupations of their creators had shifted. The experience and contacts that Arnold Schwartzman and Clive Arrowsmith had gained from designing this programme provided them with a route from the practice of graphic design in a television company to the direction of commercials and ultimately to the direction and production of feature film and documentaries.[44]

From the margins to the mainstream

Fittingly, stories of the Beatles' imminent retirement were published the same week as the announcement that the last transmission of *RSG!* would take place on 23 December 1966. Daphne Shadwell, who was called to help direct this final show, explains that 'the programme had become too big and smooth; it was getting like 'Thank Your Lucky Stars' … its spontaneity and wildness were getting lost'. On a more practical level, she remembers that 'it was getting too expensive to present the bands live'.[45] Complaints voiced by the Musicians Union, whose members were not getting enough work, led in June 1966 to the introduction of an all-out ban on television shows which allowed artists to mime to their records. *RSG!* had employed this non-miming policy on an informal basis since 1965, but the official ruling and the escalating popularity of the featured groups began to put excessive strain upon the programme's budget.

Photographic images in the national press of the bank-holiday disturbances at seaside towns during 1964 gave the mods a widespread visual tangibility and a label that entered the contemporary lexicon.[46] Similarly, by seeking to represent the verbal and visual codes of the mod subculture, *RSG!* had rendered it recognisable and, therefore, imitable.

By 1966, the mod movement, in cultural theorist Dick Hebdige's words 'subject to concerted pressures of the media, market forces and internal contradictions – between keeping private and going public – began to fracture'.[47] So *RSG!*, through its very success as a disseminator of the nuances of a mod lifestyle, played a major part in destroying its target audience. Like a quintessential pop product with concomitant expendability and built-in obsolescence, it created the conditions for its own demise. 'Not only was *RSG!* in advance of its time,' observed Melly, 'it knew when its moment was over. It was true to Pop even in this.'[48]

Notes

1 For broader discussions of the period under consideration see for instance A. Marwick's *The Sixties* (Oxford and New York: Oxford University Press, 1998) and R. Hewison's *Too Much: Art and Society in the Sixties, 1960–75* (London: Methuen, 1986).

2 N. Whiteley, *Pop Design, Modernism to Mod* (London: Design Council, 1987), p. 6.

3 John Lawton has described the notion of an establishment as one based on 'the English constitution and the group of institutions and outlying agencies built around it for its protection'. J. Lawton, *Five Hundred Days* (London: Hodder & Stoughton, 1992), p. 21.

4 A. Higgins, A. Holme and M. Masheder (eds), *Family Viewing: A Study of Early Evening Television* (London: Council of Children's Welfare, 1960).

5 T. Wolfe, *The Kandy-Kolored Tangerine-Flake Streamline Baby* (New York: Pocket Cardinal, 1966), p. 47.

6 M. Aldred, 'Our Neighbours Hate Us', *RSG! Magazine* (London, 1964), p. 23.

7 For more details of the questionnaires sent to *RSG!* viewers and interviews carried out with the individuals quoted in this chapter see A. Twemlow, 'Ready, Steady, Go!: The Evolution of a Televisual Pop-graphic Language 1963–66' (M.A. dissertation, RCA/V&A History of Design, 1996).

8 B. Sendall, *Independent TV in Britain, 1958–68*, Vol. 2 (Macmillan, 1983).

9 Questionnaire 4 from *RSG!* viewer. For details see Twemlow, 'Ready, Steady, Go!'.

10 F. Cordell, 'Gold Pan Alley: A Survey of the Popular Song Field', *Ark* (London: Royal College of Art, 1957), p. 21.

11 K. Fordyce, 'Putting Zip into the Show', *RSG!* (London: Associated Rediffusion, 1964), p. 21.

12 P. Oakes, 'Let's Go with Elkan Allen', *The Sunday Times Colour Magazine* (19 September, 1965), p. 39.

13 A great deal of scholarship centering on this period in Britain identifies the mods as a significant subcultural force. Examples include S. Hall and T. Jefferson, *Resistance Through Rituals: Youth Subcultures in Post-war Britain* (London: Hutchinson, 1975); D. Hebdige, *Subculture: The Meaning of Style* (London: Methuen, 1979), and J. Green, *All Dressed Up: The Sixties and the Counterculture* (London: Jonathan Cape, 1998).

14 'The Modelmakers', *The Sunday Times Colour Magazine*, 10 May 1964.

15 G. Melly, 'Gesture Goes Classless', *New Society*, 17 June 1965, p. 26.

16 Interview with Nicholas Ferguson, 22 September 1995. See Twemlow, 'Ready Steady, Go!'

17 Ibid.

18 Aldwych Theatre, 1962, directed by William Gaskill.

19 Interview with Nicholas Ferguson, 22 September 1995. See Twemlow, 'Ready Steady, Go!'

20 A Robert Rauschenberg exhibition took place at the Whitechapel gallery, London, during February 1964, and a Kurt Schwitters exhibition was at The Marlborough Gallery, London, March/April 1963.

21 For Dada and Surrealist artists such as Hans Arp, Max Ernst, Kurt Schwitters and Hannah Höch, the use of collage and photomontage techniques was a way of introducing fragments of the real world into art. Born out of Picasso and Braque's early experiments with 'synthetic' cubism, these artists produced disturbing avant-garde works by the juxtaposition of diverse material including scraps of newspaper, sheet music, anatomical diagrams, commercial packaging and photographs. As David Hopkins has observed, such strategies represented a departure from earlier more formalist notions of 'autonomous' art and a new attempt to examine the very nature of modern experience. In this respect, the collages that were produced were intended to serve as commentaries on contemporary life rather than as narrow expositions on art. See D. Hopkins, *Dada and Surrealism: A Very Short Introduction* (Oxford: Oxford University Press, 2004), p. 4.

22 S. Themerson, 'Kurt Schwitters on a Time Chart', *Typographica* 16 (December 1967).

23 Cordell, 'Gold Pan Alley', p. 21.

24 Interview with Nicholas Ferguson, 22 September 1995. See Twemlow, 'Ready Steady, Go!'.

25 J. McHale, 'The Expendable Ikon', *Architectural Design* (February 1959), p. 82.

26 N. Ferguson, 'Pop Goes the Artist', *Ready Steady Go! Annual* (London: TV Publications, 1965).

27 A cyclorama is a curved, stretched sky-cloth giving the impression of infinite distance, when lit.

28 R. Levin, *Television By Design* (London: Bodley Head, 1961).

29 Cordell, 'Gold Pan Alley', pp. 20–3.

30 G. Melly, *Revolt into Style: The Pop Arts in Britain* (London: Penguin, 1970), p. 167. The approach may have derived, in part, from the BBC's satirical news programme *That Was The Week That Was* which, before it ended in December 1963, had a five-month overlap with *RSG!*

31 *Ready Steady Go! Annual* (London: TV Publications, 1965).

32 Dick Lester's revolutionary use of jump-cut editing, unusual camera angles, extreme zooms, and fast and slow motion sequences in *Hard Day's Night* are described in detail in Melly, *Revolt into Style*, p. 167.

33 L. Alloway, 'The Long Front of Culture', *Cambridge Opinion* 17 (1959), pp. 25–6.

34 M. McLuhan, *The Medium is the Massage* (London: Penguin, 1967), p. 125.

35 Interview with Michael Yates 28 October 1995. See Twemlow, 'Ready Steady Go!'.

36 *Gebrauchsgraphik* (August 1960), pp. 26–34.

37 This fear of subliminal influence was part of a wider anxiety generated by McCarthyism in the USA and a rash of publications on the subject, most notably, Vance Packard's emotive text *The Hidden Persuaders*, first published by David McKay in New York in 1957, and first published in Britain by Longmans Green in 1957 and republished as a Penguin Special in 1960.

38 Interview with Arnold Schwartzman 26 October 1995. Interview with Sidney King, 28 March 1996. See Twemlow, 'Ready Steady, Go!' In the 1960s Victorian artefacts and ephemera – that had been treated reverently around the anniversary of the Great Exhibition in 1951 – began to be sampled in a more eclectic and playful manner. This trend would reach its culmination in Terry Gilliam's animated Victorian engravings for *Monty Python* in 1969. Many art directors, illustrators and designers of the period frequented an antique shop called 'Dodo Designs' opened by Robin Farrow in 1963 in Westbourne Grove. It sold commercial Victoriana such as original and reproduction enamel signs, tin boxes, labels, playbills and old lettering.

39 Clive Arrowsmith went on to be a fashion photographer, with *Vogue*, *Harpers* and *Esquire* among his clients. He also directed commercials for brands such as Heinz, Revlon and Hamlet Cigars, and music videos for artists including Jamiroquai, Jules Holland, and Def Leppard. Arnold Schwartzman moved to Los Angeles and directed films and documentaries in addition to running his graphic design practice. He won an Oscar in 1982 for his documentary feature *Genocide*.

40 Clive Arrowsmith, the designer of this sequence, often did commissions for Tom Wolsey and it was one of these that secured him his job at Rediffusion. Interview with Clive Arrowsmith, 27 March 1996.

41 D. Davis, *The Grammar of TV Production* (London: Guild of TV Producers and Directors, 1966).

42 Interview with Arnold Schwartzman 26 October 1995. See Twemlow, 'Ready Steady, Go!'.

43 C. Booker, *The Neophiliacs: The Revolution on English Life in the Fifties and Sixties* (London: Pimlico, 1992, originally published 1969), p. 56.

44 Similarly, Nicholas Ferguson, the set designer, also went on to become a director of dramatic productions and pop videos. Interview with Ferguson, 22 September 1995. See Twemlow, 'Ready Steady, Go!'

45 Ibid. Interview with Daphne Shadwell and John P. Hamilton, 8 January 1995.

46 R. Barnes, *Mods!* (London: Plexus, 1991).

47 D. Hebdige, *Subculture and the Meaning of Style* (London: Methuen, 1979), p. 52.

48 Melly, *Revolt into Style*, p. 171.

Index

Figures in **bold** refer to illustrations.